The Life and Work of an Atheist Pioneer

The Life and Work of an Atheist Pioneer

Christos Tzanetakos

iUniverse, Inc.
Bloomington

The Life and Work of an Atheist Pioneer

iUniverse books may be ordered through booksellers or by contacting:

iUniverse
1663 Liberty Drive
Bloomington, IN 47403
www.iuniverse.com
1-800-Authors (1-800-288-4677)

ISBN: 978-1-4620-4499-3 (sc)
ISBN: 978-1-4620-4498-6 (hc)
ISBN: 978-1-4620-4497-9 (ebk)

Library of Congress Control Number: 2011916158

Printed in the United States of America

iUniverse rev. date: 08/30/2011

Contents

To

Alice

Chapter 1

The Early Years

I was born on December 23, 1938. At the time, my parents and siblings were living in Stavroupolis, a small city at the northeastern part of Greece known as Thrake, where my military father was stationed.

The custom for Greek parents was to give their firstborn sons the names of their grandfathers. My oldest brother, Anastasios, got his name from the grandfather on our father's side, and my second-oldest brother was named Leonidas for the grandfather on our mother's side.

Born just before Christmas, I was named Christos (in Greek "Χρηστος") after the alleged founder of the Christian religion. The name later became very ironic because in my teen years I rejected the Greek Orthodox religion my parents and the Greek culture and government had forced upon me and eventually became a critic of all religions as untrue, superstitious, and harmful to life on our planet.

I was not even a year old in 1939 when Hitler's war drums began reverberating through Europe. My father was in the Greek army and foresaw the danger of what became World War II. He sent his family to his birthplace of Laconia, the mythic valley of Sparta in the Peloponnese peninsula.

For a short time my mother, Georgia, and all her five children (me, my two brothers, and two sisters) stayed in a village named Socha situated high on the slopes of Mount Taygetos. Conditions in this village were primitive, with no electricity, running water, or any other amenities.

Soon after, my mother moved the family to my father's village called Amykles, a picturesque place among orange and olive groves, vineyards, and fertile fields down in the valley. It was only a few miles from Sparta, the capital of the region.

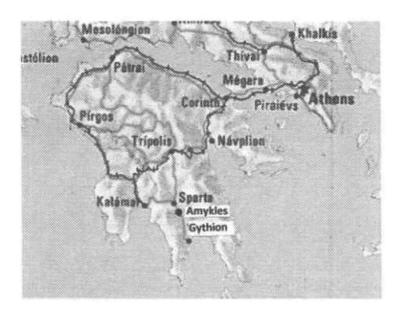

Amykles was inhabited by only a few hundred people and like all the Greek villages in the 1940s had no electricity or running water.

It was here that I took my first steps and started my exploration of life.

Although the world was embroiled in World War II, life in Amykles was still peaceful for me. I was too young to be affected by the war and enjoyed the beauty of the bucolic valley of Laconia.

Front row left to right, brother Louis, sister Anna, brother Tassos and sister Voula.
Back row left to right, Me held by my mother Georgia, a family relative.

Although World War II ended in 1945, for Greece the insanity of war continued and in 1946 a civil war erupted. The war lasted until 1949 and further ravaged the country with untold misery, tragedies, and atrocities.

The conflict was between communists (adherents to the philosophy of communism for equality among the people), who had many intellectuals among their leaders, and the so-called nationalists, who blindly supported the doctrine of the divine kings and the established powerful Greek Orthodox Church.

However, some of the Greek priests supported the communist army, and ironically both armies had their weapons blessed by the same "god" to kill each other.

Childhood in Amykles was full of adventures. Since my father, Dimitrios, was fighting in the wars, my siblings and I helped our mother cope with life in the country.

My mother was a very dynamic and intelligent woman. In spite of her limited education, she succeeded in keeping the family healthy and most importantly happy during our years in Amykles.

With my mother Georgia and big brother Tassos from the years in Amykles

When my parents were married, they bought an orange grove in Amykles. The grove had 170 orange trees and an empty parcel with a big mulberry tree. It was on this parcel where we planted our vegetables (tomatoes, lettuce, eggplant, corn, potatoes, etc.) and kept two sheep and a goat that provided us with fresh milk for drinking and making feta cheese.

The house our family rented had a yard with orange trees, fig trees, grapevines, and other fruit trees. My mother bought a few chickens and a rooster and let them nest their eggs. Pretty soon the yard was full of fluffy little chirping chicks. With the help of relatives, a chicken coop was built and in time the number of chickens grew to almost a hundred, providing an abundance of fresh eggs and poultry.

The memories from the life in Amykles are etched in my brain. Life was very interesting, adventurous, and challenging.

Our family had to learn new skills and invent ways to survive. One very important commodity was soap, which was hard to get then in the village. We saved all the used olive oil and any animal fats in clay pots, and when we had enough, my mother borrowed a big cauldron from the villagers to make soap.

A young boy by then, I remember going with my mother to Sparta to get potassium, the other ingredient necessary to make soap. Back in the village my mother would place the oils, fats, and potassium in the cauldron and boil them for long time, stirring the mixture with a long wooden spoon-like instrument to avoid breathing the poisonous fumes emanating from the top of the cauldron. When a thick layer formed on the surface, she let it cool for a day and then removed the thick crust and cut it in small soap bars. The family now had enough soap until next year's production.

When I was six years old, my mother bought me a slate and a slate pencil for my first year in school. Of course, paper and pencils as we have today were not available in the village. I had to learn my ABCs on the slate. The first day of school was not a very pleasant one; I dropped my slate in the schoolyard and broke it. I returned home in tears and expected to be scolded. When my mother saw her always happy boy in tears, she hugged me and promised to get me a new slate.

5

I loved school, and although I was not very studious (like all boys, I preferred to play outdoors climbing trees, hunting birds and small animals with my slingshot, and setting traps), I excelled in my studies, which made my mother very proud.

Without electricity, the nights were dark, and I had to do my homework and read my book by an oil lamp.

Oil lamp similar to the one we used in Amykles

Olive oil was not only very important for cooking; its use was for light and medicinal purposes.

During the years at Amykles, my brothers, sisters, and I participated in all the seasonal events, such as harvesting the orange groves, olive groves, and the vineyards. Harvesting the vineyards was the most fun because after picking the grapes, we would crush the grapes by jumping around barefooted in a shallow pool-like place where the grapes had been dumped.

Stomping on the grapes

The juice from the crushed grapes was drained to an underground reservoir and from there to wine barrels that all villagers had in their cellars. They let the juice in the barrels ferment for a while, and then the barrels were sealed for a year to produce the next season's wine. The barrels were made from oak to give the wine a special taste. Most of them had been in the cellars for generations.

Wine barrel

The children also loved the vineyards' harvest season because the mothers use the juice to make cookies and a special delicacy with walnuts. They boiled the juice with honey, flour, and some other ingredients to form a thick pudding-like chocolate. Then they dipped strings of walnuts until they were covered with layers of the pudding.

When the pudding covering the walnuts was thick enough, they let them dry in the air to harden like chocolate. The candy was delicious and nutritious as well.

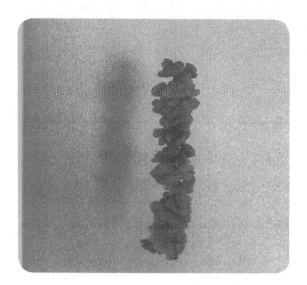 

String with walnuts

Covered walnuts

The orange groves harvest was also fun for the children during the German occupation of the country, although very disconcerting for the growers. With the war on, trade with the big cities had been halted, and the oranges were piled in mountains and rotting. It became a source of play. The village was divided by a main road into the north and south village, and the kids from each side waged "war" against each other using the rotting oranges for ammunition. The event was exciting without any serious injuries.

When the olives were ready to be harvested, my siblings and I helped pick them not only to produce the delicious olive oil for cooking, but to make cracked and Kalamata-type olives. My favorite was the cracked green olives that my mother made.

2010/01/11

Cracked green olives

After picking the green olives, the whole family was busy preparing the olives for curing. We cracked the olives with a flat stone, and when we had enough for the year, we placed them in a tub with water and salt to be cured. After several changes of the water and salt (brine), the bitterness from the green olives was gone. Then my mother would add spices, place the cured olives in pots, and fill them with fresh olive oil. The family had now olives to last them until the next year's harvest. Through the year were events that made life interesting and exciting, at least for the children. There were animal fairs, festivals for church name celebrations, and weddings, and even some of the funerals (when the dead were old) were cases for celebration.

Helping and contributing to our family's needs was also a source of fun and adventure. We obtained walnuts and chestnuts from wild trees on the slopes of Mount Taygetos. The fruits were free for the taking, and the village kids and I had a field day collecting them. On winter days (winters were very mild in the valley of Laconia) after a rain, the children would search for snails (escargot) and edible mushrooms.

Escargot

Other sources of food were edible plants and berries. My siblings and I collected the dandelions and wild greens and blackberries that were plentiful around the village.

Dandelion   Zochos greens (hogweed)   Blackberries

The valley of Laconia was the stopover for many migrating birds on their way from Northern Europe to Africa. By then I had become an expert marksman with the slingshot and very skillful at setting traps. I provided the family with bird and small animal game.

Another fun chore was collecting fresh leaves from mulberry trees for the silkworms. Practically all the villagers grew silkworms, which had to be fed with plenty of mulberry leaves.

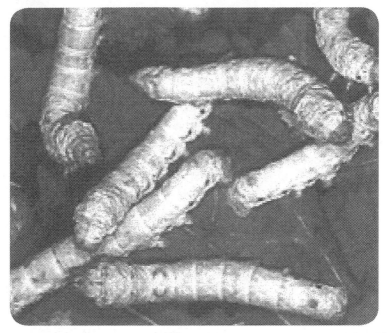

Silkworms

The silkworms were placed on flat beds made out of canes, and for weeks they devoured the fresh leaves before they formed a cocoon. When the cocoons were ready to open for the silk butterflies to come out, the villagers took the cocoons and boiled them in big cauldrons. I didn't like this because the stench from the boiling cocoons was awful.

Despite the many hours the other kids in the village and I spent on chores, we had plenty of time for fun and games.

We played war games, throwing stones at the opposite teams by hand or with slingshots. This was a very dangerous game that resulted in many head wounds and other serious injuries. Of course, the grownups never approved of it. Girls also played the game, but their duties were to take care of the wounded.

Other games we played were hide and seek and a blindfold version where the blindfolded person had to guess who was in front of him or her. (That was favored by the boys who had to guess which girl was there). Marbles and spinning tops were also popular among the boys. My pockets were always full.

Marbles

The village boys made their own toys. The most popular was made out of an iron bar bent into a ring like today's plastic hula hoops. Rims from bicycles, tires, or any similar item were also used. The ring was pushed and guided by a bar with a handle on one end and a U shape at the other. The U end was placed a little lower than the middle point. We would spend hours pushing this toy through the village streets.

My childhood toy

We also made kites, hot air balloons, rockets, and firecrackers. The kites were made using shaved pieces of cane to form a hexagonal frame tied with string. A thin paper was glued with homemade glue made out of flour and water. A tail and the balancing strings were added, and the kite was ready to fly.

Homemade kite

The hot air balloons were made with a round rim of about two feet in diameter with two cross sections. A thin paper balloon was glued around the rim, and a rag saturated with oil was tied in the center of the cross. A boy would hold the balloon from a wall, and then the oil would be ignited. The smoke and hot air from the fire would fill the balloon, and it would start to rise in the air. A swarm of boys and girls would follow the balloon as it was carried by the winds for miles until the oil was burned, and the balloon would start to fall.

Sometimes the balloon would land on roofs with the oil still burning and cause fires. As far as I remember, there was never any serious damage.

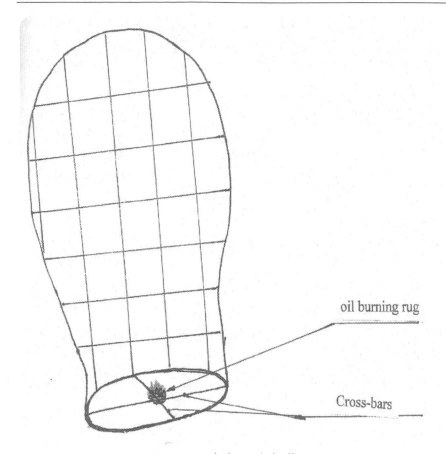

oil burning rug

Cross-bars

Homemade hot air balloon

The rockets were made using an empty can that was open at the bottom and had a small hole in the center of the top. A hole the size of the can's diameter was dug in the ground and filled halfway with water. A few pieces of dry acetylene were added to the hole, and we immediately placed the can with the bottom with the hole up close to the surface of the ground and sealed it with mud. In a few minutes, the acetylene in the water would produce flammable vapors. Then one of the kids, holding a long stick with a burning rug, would place it close to the hole, and the fire would ignite the vapors inside the can. There would be a loud explosion, and the can would fly up in the air to a great height. The village kids and even the adults would applaud.

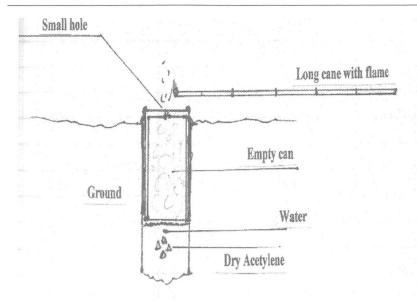

Acetylene-fueled can rocket

Firecrackers were made by the older kids of the village. They placed powder in a triangle-shaped paper similar to the spinach triangles mothers made with phyllo dough. In one corner they attached a fuse made of flammable material. After igniting the fuse, they had to toss the firecracker away before it exploded.

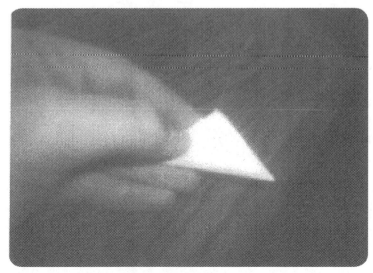

Triangle firecracker

One time some village kids secretly placed firecrackers in the Thymiato (an incensory, which is an instrument that the Greek priests use to incense the faithful) during an Easter Mass celebration. When the priest tossed the incensory around the faithful, the firecrackers caught fire and exploded, creating pandemonium in the church and leaving the priest fuming, the adults making the sign of the cross in astonishment, and the kids having a big laugh. As far as I remember, they never caught the perpetrators.

Thymiato (incensory)

Our years in Amykles came to an end in 1947, when my father sent for the family to join him.

With World War II already over and the Greek civil war leaning toward a victory for the nationalists (if anyone can call the outcome of any war, especially a civil war, a victory), he felt it was now safe for the family to leave Amykles and move to the town of Thessaloniki, where he was stationed. We packed our belongings, sold or gave away whatever we couldn't take with us, and went to the port city of Gythio a few miles from Amykles to board a small freighter that would take us to Thessaloniki.

The quaint port city of Gythio   From Gythio to Thessaloniki

For me, a boy of nine years old, leaving friends, relatives, the beloved grounds of Amykles, the beautiful valley of Laconia with the Evrotas River, where I had played in the shallow pools with the other kids of the village and learned how to swim, and the majestic Mount Taygetos, where I had hiked and explored the forest, was heartbreaking.

The voyage from Gythio to Thessaloniki, located in the northern part of Greece, on the small freighter was an ordeal, for we met some very rough seas and came very close to a shipwreck. My family and most all other passengers aboard became very seasick.

Eventually, the freighter entered the calm waters of the Thermaikos Gulf, and I had my first glimpse of the beautiful city of Thessaloniki. Here was where I would reach adolescence, develop my character, and formulate my early ideas of life and our cosmos. I would now start the next stage of my life.

Though I mourned for Amykles, when I saw the great sea and the vista of Thessaloniki as the freighter approached the harbor, I was enthralled with the prospect of the new beginning.

Thessaloniki, with its landmark tower

The city of Thessaloniki was founded around 315 BC by Cassander, king of Macedonia. He named it after his wife Thessaloniki, a half-sister of Alexander the Great. It is the second largest city of Greece after Athens.

When my family arrived, the city had a population of about 300,000 to 400,000 inhabitants. The city had electricity, running water, and plumbing in contrast to the rather primitive conditions of Amykles. We settled in an apartment close to the seaside, where I would later become an avid fisherman, providing the family with fresh fish from the sparkling clear waters of the Thermaikos Gulf. Unfortunately, the Gulf would later be polluted as Thessaloniki developed into a heavily industrialized area with a population of over a million.

I was enrolled in the 12th ELEMENTARY SCHOOL of Thessaloniki, a beautiful school surrounded by a large dirt field. The field was the playground where my new classmates and I would play soccer and other games. I was now a third grader.

My class at the 12th ELEMENTARY SCHOOL of Thessaloniki. I am the fifth boy from right to left in the second row from top.

Christos

The elementary school in Thessaloniki (1995)

Forty-eight years later, on my yearly visits to Greece with my wife, Alice, the school still stands, but the playground around it has been transformed to paved streets with parked cars on both sides.

On my first day of school, which had already started when I was enrolled, the teacher introduced me as the new Spartan boy. This was an introduction that would have a very strong influence on my character and behavior. Fully aware of my famous warrior ancestors, I would apply myself to the Spartan principles. Although I was not of big stature, I was undefeated in wrestling and other games among the other boys of my age and even older

From the ancient Spartan culture and history, I developed self-discipline and respect for my elders. The stories of how the Spartan youth would offer their places to the elders of the city during the games (similar to the Olympics) and other events were deeply rooted in my brain. On public transportation, I would offer my seat or assist the elderly, feeling proud and self-gratified.

In my father's army jeep (1949)

Life in the big city was exciting. I discovered the movies and my lifelong love for books. The French author Jules Verne, precursor of modern science fiction and scientific technology, ignited my imagination and sparked my first scientific inquiries with his books

The Mysterious Island, Twenty Thousand Leagues Under the Sea, From the Earth to the Moon, Around the World in Eighty Days, and others that were translated to Greek.

Another French author, Hector Malot, with his books *Nobody's Boy* and *Nobody's Girl,* aroused my compassion for the underprivileged and destitute children of the world. I also discovered the American author Mark Twain. His books *Adventures of Tom Sawyer, Adventures of Huckleberry Finn, A Connecticut Yankee in King Arthur's Court, The Prince and the Pauper,* and others gave me many hours of pleasure and led me to question and scrutinize 'the institutions of government and religion.

Many years later, when I immigrated to the United States, I founded a scholarship fund organization to assist young university students in paying for tuition and books. I named this organization The Mark Twain Scholarship Fund in honor of my beloved author.

Finally, the Greek author Nikos Kazantzakis removed all the religious superstitious cobwebs from my brain, and I totally rejected the Greek Christian Orthodox religion. In my mid-teen years I became a free thinker, and later, when I studied all the major religions of humankind, I would reject them as ludicrous, primitive, and unscientific superstitions. Eventually I adhered to the philosophy of atheism and proudly proclaimed myself an atheist.

Nikos Kazantzakis was also a big influence on my love for traveling.

After reading his travel books *Journey to Morea, Spain, England, Japan, China,* and others, I would dream of visiting all these places, which eventually became a reality. Years later, I visited Nikos Kazantzakis's tomb in Crete and was thrilled to read his epitaph:

I hope for nothing. I fear nothing. I am free.

In Thessaloniki, I became a movie enthusiast, a passion that continues today. In my early teens, the movies I loved the most were the Tarzan series with Johnny Weismuller and Maureen O'Sullivan, buccaneer movies, cowboy movies, spy movies, and other adventurous films like *Robin Hood* and *The Mark of Zorro.*

To save money for the movies, I would walk to school, which was a few miles from home, instead of taking a tram or bus.

The cowboy movies were all Hollywood made, and they depicted the American Indians as the villains. Many years later, I would read *The Indian Wars* and *Bury My Heart at Wounded Knee.*

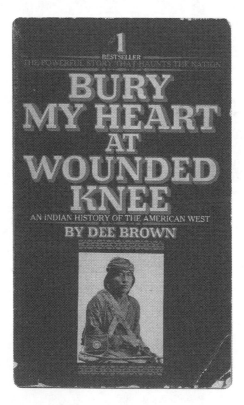

By then of course I had realized that the American movie industry was part and parcel with the official American propaganda machine, which distorted history in its favor'.

I graduated with honors from the 12th ELEMENTARY SCHOOL of Thessaloniki, which was compulsory. As the school system in Greece required, I took the exams for entrance to high school or gymnasium, as it was named, for the next six years of my education. I passed the exams effortlessly, and I was admitted to the Fifth Boy's Gymnasium (gymnasiums, also known as high schools, were segregated between boys and girls).

The Fifth Boy's Gymnasium of Thessaloniki
(The book cover of the famous school)

The Fifth Boy's Gymnasium gained its fame thanks to a charismatic and dedicated educator under whose leadership and guidance the school attracted students not only from Thessaloniki, but from other cities as well. His name was Stefanos Kotsiras, and although very strict, he inspired his staff of teachers and, most importantly, all of the students to do their best. To be a student at the Fifth Gymnasium was a privilege and a joy.

Stefanos Kotsiras

In 1951, a graduate named Nikolaos Meligopoulos, who later became a doctor, wrote a poem for the beloved school, and the music teacher Antonios Kazantzis composed the music for it. It became the official anthem of the Fifth Boy's Gymnasium of Thessaloniki.

Anthem of the Fifth Boy's Gymnasium

We are the youth of Greece
The gallant students of the Fifth Gymnasium
that we hold deep in our hearts
the heavy heritage of Greece.
With confidence rooted strong in our hearts
with an immense flame in our breasts
workers in our great aspirations
with pure knowledge and noble culture.

And now with enthusiasm,
let us all labor together
to lift our Fifth gymnasium
and all with joy let us wrestle
our dream to justly become true.

The building is now owned by the National Bank of Greece and serves as a cultural center. It mounts exhibitions, holds lectures, shows films, and liaises with other cultural institutions in Thessaloniki. My class visits our beloved Gymnasium on class reunions.

My class with some of our teachers (1955)   Christos
I am the fourth boy from left to right in the second row
from top.

Most of the boys from my elementary school entered the Fifth Boy's Gymnasium, and I was happy to have my friends with me. During my time there, I shared the same desk with my friend Dimitrios Tsinidis, a boy from a poor family whose mother was a widow and with whom I have remained friends. The two of us as a team would wrestle (back to back) with the other boys, and we were undefeated. I visit my friends and classmates in Thessaloniki whenever Alice and I travel to Greece. Dimitrios (or Mimis, as was his nickname) and I reminisce and even took a photo posing back to back as we had done when young.

With my childhood friend Mimis Tsinidis,
October 2009

Although I live 5,000 nautical miles away from Greece and Thessaloniki, I attend the class reunions held every five years.

With some of my classmates at our 2003 reunion.
I am the fourth in the first row, from left to right.

By now the civil war was over and my father, a decorated lieutenant colonel whose battalion had captured the last strong hold of the communists on Mount Pindos thus ending the shameful war, returned to Thessaoniki and the family. He was appointed commander of the military units in Thessaloniki and its territory. I would accompany him often to the army outposts for inspections and enjoyed the privileges and attention I received.

With my father and army personnel

It was now the 1950s, and I discovered other interests besides books, movies, and games. My mind was now preoccupied with girls and my personal appearance. I began combing my hair and carrying a comb everywhere in my pocket, and I asked my parents for long trousers and a three-piece suit.

My Greek ID issued in 1954

At this time I also became interested in world politics and philosophical matters. World War II had caused an estimated death toll of sixty-two to seventy-eight million, making it the deadliest war ever. In Greece, the civil war had compounded the destruction with an additional 150,000 deaths. European countries as well as Japan and the Far East were left in ruins. Yet I thought humankind did not learn much.

In spite of the formation in 1945 of the United Nations and the 1948 adoption of the noble Declaration of Universal Human Rights, the world was still in turmoil and would remain the same for decades to come. Fanatical political ideologies backed by religious beliefs had created the so-called Cold War between the two superpowers of the time, with the United States and its allies on one side and Russia and her allies on the other. After the defeat of the communist army, Greece, an ally of the United States, became a police state. The political and military leaders of the communist party who survived were persecuted and prosecuted in kangaroo courts no better than the Holy Inquisition's. They were sentenced to hard labor in concentration camps where every form of torture and degradation was inflicted upon them. The communist party, of course, was outlawed. So much for freedom of thought and expression in the country that gave birth to the ideas of democracy and freedom.

The powerful police issued certificates of conformity (**πιστοποιητικό κοινωνικών φρονημάτων),** which were required by all the citizens if they applied for any position remotely connected to the government or the educational system. Because of this paranoia, a large number of Greek people were denied work not only in the government but in many private enterprises as well.

This shameful practice was suspended in the mid-fifties, but the paranoia was still around when, in 1961, I was called to serve in the Greek Royal Navy. Prior to my acceptance in the Royal Navy, all the draftees were interviewed (interrogated) by an officer who asked:

"Are the communists good people or bad people?"

I answered that in my opinion, people are good or bad regardless of their political or religious convictions. The officer, seeing from his file that I was the son of a well-known army officer, was surprised by my answer, but after further questioning, he accepted my arguments. I served on the Royal Navy destroyer ΔΟΞΑ (Glory) for two-and-a-half years.

The destroyer ΔΟΞΑ (*Glory*)   Me as commissioned officer

A pacifist by now, I thought the Navy years were a waste of time. They further reinforced my conviction that national armies should be abolished and world conflicts should be addressed and solved by the United Nations through diplomacy, or, if necessary, by an international force under the aegis of the United Nations.

I was impressed by the small country of Costa Rica, which in 1948 abolished its military. In 1986, Costa Rican president Oscar Arias declared December 1 the Military Abolition Day. In 1990, when Alice, our daughter, Georgia, and I were in Paris, we met Oscar Arias with his family strolling down Avenue des Champs-Elysees. Alice and I were thrilled to shake hands with him. Oscar Arias was the 1987 recipient of the Nobel Peace prize.

For me, the 1950s was a decade of searching and reflection. They were years of rebellion and further questioning the sanity of our species. Notwithstanding the small country of Costa Rica, the world was more militaristic than ever, and the arms race, especially the nuclear weapons, threatened total annihilation of both humankind and life itself.

After studying both Greek and world history, I came to realize that history books were biased and reflected the views of their authors and the sponsoring governments. I opposed the perpetuation of hate between Greece and its neighbors Turkey and Bulgaria as it was depicted in the Greek history texts.

Other events in the 1950s that influenced me were the struggles of indigenous peoples around the globe against colonial powers, especially the British and the French. In my youth, I idolized Mahatma Gandhi who, by peaceful resistance, defeated the British rule and freed India from their tyranny. Mahatma Gandhi was assassinated by a Muslim fanatic in 1948.

In 1952, I sympathized with the Mau Mau movement to free Kenya from the British rule, and years later I would quote in my writings the first president of free Kenya, Jomo Kenyatta, who, referring to the Christian missionaries in Africa, stated:

> When the Missionaries arrived, the Africans had the land and the Missionaries had the Bible. They taught how to pray with our eyes closed. When we opened them, they had the land and we had the Bible.

Another British atrocity that infuriated me as well as all the Greeks was the hanging execution on May 10, 1956, of two young men in Cyprus. The hanged revolutionaries Karaolis and Dimitriou became the national martyrs of Cyprus, which eventually shook off the British yoke.

The paranoia of the threat of communism was prevalent in the United States as well. It was in the 1950s that I heard on the radio and read in the newspapers of the insanity of McCarthyism. McCarthyism was the political persecution of American intellectuals, artists, and others with liberal views. These people suffered many indignities and lost their livelihoods as a result of the actions of Senator Joseph Raymond McCarthy and his committee of mostly Christian lunatic fanatics.

The 1950s was the decade of many other wars around the globe, including the Korean War and the beginning of the most shameful war of all, the Vietnam War. In 1955, the United States agreed to train the South Vietnamese army and eventually got fully involved in the war. By the end of the Vietnam War, the toll in American lives was 58,159 dead and thousands maimed physically and mentally for life. The destruction and death of the Vietnamese people and the surrounding countries of Laos and Cambodia bombed by the Americans was incalculable. The Vietnamese casualties were estimated between 3 to 4 million and the Laotians and Cambodians between 1.5 to 2 million.

Many years later, when Alice and I moved to North Hutchinson Island in Florida, we visited the National Navy UDT Seal Museum, situated only two blocks from our condominium. The museum is the actual place where a special commando unit of the American army was used to train its members to perform underwater demolitions. They were named SEALS.

Among the exhibits was a video depicting the actions of the SEALS in Vietnam. When a gruesome photo of a row of dead Vietnamese appeared on the screen, the narrator proudly stated that for every one SEAL killed by the North Vietnamese, the SEALS's comrades would go out and slaughter 300 Vietnamese for reprisal.

I questioned the curator of the museum (a former SEAL) if he realized that this practice was copied from the German army in occupied Europe during World War II, which executed a number of locals for each German soldier killed by the resistance. The number of the German executions was much smaller than the 300 for each SEAL.

I said to the curator, "Don't you think that the Vietnamese who were fighting to free their country from foreign powers had parents, wives, and children?"

"How ironic," I continued, "that the descendants of the American Revolution, who fought to gain their independence from the British, were now fighting against other peoples' struggle for independence."

The Vietnam War was a war for independence. Vietnam was colonized by the French in 1857 and remained under their occupation until World War II, when Japan occupied the country until the end of the war in 1945. The French resumed their colonization from 1946 to 1953 when the Vietnamese, under the leadership of Ho Chi Minh, defeated them and the country was divided into North and South Vietnam. South Vietnam was supported by the United States and the Catholic Church (the French had converted the Vietnamese to Catholicism), and the North was supported by Communist China.

What we now call the Vietnam War was the effort of North Vietnam to unify the country and expel the corrupt government from the South. The war ended with the defeat of the American and South Vietnamese forces.

I remembered what Albert Einstein said:

> Learn from yesterday, live for today, hope for tomorrow. The important thing is not to stop questioning.

I also noticed what Mark Twain wrote about man and wars:

> Man is the only animal that deals in that atrocity of atrocities, War. He is the only one that gathers his brethren about him and goes forth in cold blood and calm pulse to exterminate his kind. He is the only animal that for sordid wages will march out . . . and help to slaughter strangers of his own species who have done him no harm and with whom he has no quarrel . . . .
>
> And in the intervals between campaigns he washes the blood off his hands and works for 'the universal brotherhood of man'—with his mouth.

Finally, the lyrics of John Lennon's song "Imagine" came to my mind.

Nothing to kill or die for
And no religion too
Imagine all the people . . .
Sharing all the world

All in all, for me the years in the beautiful city of Thessaloniki were happy and productive. My thirst for learning was encouraged by the competitive ambience of my gymnasium and my teachers who brought new interests and goals. My favorite subjects were mathematics, physics, and chemistry, and I was a top student in all of them. I was not very good in ancient Greek literature because we spent a lot of time memorizing the ancient text, a practice that I thought was boring and a waste of time and energy. I felt it would have been more beneficial if we were taught the ancient Greek classics from translations in modern Greek.

Another subject that I barely passed was French. At that time, French was the language of commerce and diplomacy, and it was compulsory for all the gymnasium years. When I reached the fifth year, the school system changed the rules, and students had the opportunity to choose between the Department of Classics and the Department of Science for the last two years of gymnasium. The classics were more intense in literature and the science department in physics, mathematics, and chemistry. I chose the latter.

The new curriculum of physics and chemistry became more interesting for me with the additional classes in the laboratories. The labs, although not very elaborate due to lack of funds, were where I spent most of my pleasant hours in school.

While life in school and among friends was happy and contented; my family had its problems.

Once the wars were over, my father and mother got into a lot of arguments. After the many years away in wars, my father was not conditioned for a domestic family life; nevertheless, they remained together, and they had their good and bad times.

Another calamity that struck the family was the illness of my eldest brother Tassos. He had tuberculosis, or consumption as it was commonly known, which caused the most widespread public concern not only in Greece, but in all Europe and around the world. The disease was very contagious.

My parents, afraid for the other children, had Tassos admitted to a sanatorium, where he remained for several years and almost died. Finally, an effective treatment and cure became possible with the development of the antibiotic Streptomycin. Although cured of tuberculosis, Tassos remained a hypochondriac and a religious fanatic for the rest of his life. His religious irrationality would credit his cure to God and the myriad of saints of the Greek Orthodox religion. He spent the rest of his life worshiping God and the saints in spite of his cure by the wonders of science. Years later, when his only daughter (born with mental retardation) was choked to death trying to swallow A candy, he was still praising the irrational concept of God.

Our family was now together again and we resided in the first floor of a magnificent villa owned by the government. The top floor was occupied by an army general and his family. The villa is now a municipal art gallery. Years later, I took Alice to see the beautiful building.

Villa Mondoch, today a municipal art gallery Alice on
the steps of my family's home in Thessaloniki during
our travels to Greece.

In 1954, my father retired from the army, and in that year the government established a housing development for army families in a new suburb of Athens named Papagos as a tribute to the field marshal of the Greek army who won the war. My family finally had our own house, and once more we had to say good-bye to friends and acquaintances when we moved to Athens.

All of my life I have remembered Thessaloniki, the place of my youth and many fond memories, and I visit the beloved city to meet with childhood friends as often as conditions allow. We moved to Athens by train, and I found myself again in a new environment. The new house was one story with a small yard, a stone wall fence, and a flat roof with a view of Athens and the Acropolis.

With brothers Louis and Tassos at the Acropolis in Athens

In the next few years, the roof would become the place of many parties.

Dancing the night away at the Papagos home in Athens

The new suburb of Papagos was a few kilometers from downtown Athens, and the last bus service was at midnight, resuming again at six in the morning. Since nobody had a car then, the parties would start in the evening and last until morning when the partygoers were able to get a bus home. If it rained, the parties would be indoors. (My parents were very cooperative.)

I was enrolled in the 10th Gymnasium of Athens, where I completed the last year of gymnasium. In 1956, the Greek government established a new Merchant Marine Academy to meet the needs of the flourishing Merchant Marine fleet (the second in the world) with a large amount of money donated by Greek shipowners (Greece is a maritime country with a history going back to ancient times).

A sea lover from my years in Thessaloniki, I entered the exams for candidacy. The Academy had two schools—the school for captains and the school for marine engineering. I applied to the engineering school, successfully passed the exams, and became one of the sixty students of the new engineering academy.

My ID from the Merchant Marine Academy

I spent the next three years living at the Merchant Marine Academy of Aspropyrgos. Aspropyrgos was the site where the new academy was established, some twenty kilometers from Athens.

The buildings of the New Merchant Marine Academy

The new academy was situated on several acres with new buildings for classrooms, administration offices, dormitories, dining and recreation rooms, an infirmary, and cooking facilities.

The academy building with the classrooms and offices

In addition to the main buildings, the engineering school had a building with workshops, machine tools, diesel and steam turbines, boilers, and other machinery and instruments.

Practicing on lathe machine
(I am at the second lath machine)

For the captain's school, there was a building by the small marina that housed the navigation instruments, rowboats, equipment, etc. Sailboats and rowboats were anchored in the small marina and were shared with the engineering students who had lessons in marine navigation and rowing practice as well.

Rowing practice
(I am in the back in the fourth row from front)

The academy had a track and soccer field and a set of basketball courts. Soccer and basketball were the most popular sports in Greece. I played a lot of soccer and some basketball there.

At soccer practice, I am the third from left

The years in the academy were exciting. I was in the environment I had always wanted. Besides the knowledge that the academy provided, I enjoyed the dances at the school's recreation hall.

With sisters Anna, second from left, sister Voula, second from right, and classmates

With sister Anna at an academy ball

Another pleasure for me was the training trips on the academy's sailing ship. The trips would take place during the summer season when the regular classes were over, and the small schooner took me and my classmates all around the beautiful Greek islands.

Away on a trip (I am on left)

Washing the decks
(I'm holding the hose)

Years later, I would take Alice to visit all the familiar islands dotted with the quaint villages, beautiful harbors, and of course the outdoor tavernas with delicious Greek cuisine.

Me and Alice during a trip to the Greek Islands.
(Alice admires the octopus)

As the academy years came to an end, I was restless and anxious to start my seafaring career. In 1959, the first class of engineers of the new academy was inspected by Paul, the king of Greece, and we received our diplomas.

The inspection of the first class of the academy by King Paul.
I am the first in the first row.

I was among the top ten students of my class and selected by Papadakis Marine Shipping company, which invited me to be employed on its vessels as apprentice engineer. I accepted the offer.

In July 1959, I said good-bye to my family, sweetheart, and friends and entered the seafaring chapter of my life, which would take me around the world for the next ten years. On August 19, 1959, with a letter of introduction from the general manager of Papadakis Maritime Company, I boarded a passenger vessel from Piraeus bound for the port of Alexandria in Egypt. My seafaring years had begun.

Chapter 2

Alice

Alice, whose Greek name is Arete, was born in 1935 in Pittsburgh, Pennsylvania. She was the youngest of six children born to Christos and Maria-Tzamouzakis Stambolis.

Alice's family photo: From left, sister Helen, mother Maria with Alice on her lap, brother Constantine (Gus), Father Christos Stambolis with sister Theodora in front, and sister Sophia. Missing from the photo is brother Angelo.

Alice had two brothers, Angelo and Constantine (Gus), and three sisters, Helen, Sophia, and Theodora. Her father, Christos Stambolis, was born of Greek parents in Braila, a harbor city on the Danube River in Romania. Later, he moved to Asia Minor (now Turkey), and from there he came to the United States in the early 1920s. He was introduced to his wife Maria. Their marriage was arranged by relatives as was the custom of their time. Alice's mother Maria was the only girl of eight siblings.

Alice's Greek name *Arete* in English means *virtue*. The name has its origin in the ancient Greek mythology where Virtue or Arete was the goddess of virtue, excellence, goodness, and valor. When I met her in 1969 in Miami, Florida, I was captivated by her and later convinced that besides her million dollar smile and good looks, Alice possessed all that her namesake is credited for.

According to Greek mythology, when the hero Hercules left home to start his legendary life, he met at a fork of the road Arete and her counterpart Kakia, or the goddess of easy pleasures. They offered him a choice between a pleasant and easy life and a severe but glorious life: he chose the latter. Similar to Hercules, I also chose Arete, and I never regretted it.

Alice's education was limited to a high school diploma, but to me her intellect and critical thinking is superior to most holders of university degrees.

Early in her life, clear thinking freed her from the stale and superstitious Greek mentality of her parents and relatives in Pittsburgh. She also escaped the Greek Orthodox religion of her parents, which she found as irrational and laughable as all other religions.

When I accompanied Alice to her fiftieth high school class reunion, I found out from her male schoolmates that practically all of them were in love with her. She of course was one of the beauties in her class.

Alice about ten years old   Alice in her teens with her dog Duchess

When Alice captured me

Alice's childhood was a happy one. Since she was the youngest of all the nieces and nephews, she was pampered and literally spoiled by her uncles. She was also pampered by her godmother Arete Giannakakis, who, not having children of her own, devoted all her love and affection to Alice and became her second mother.

Although her early years among Greek relatives and the Greek community where they lived was happy, when time came for young Arete to go to school, she found herself an alien among the other American kids. The only language she knew was Greek.

When Alice graduated from Swissvale High School in 1954, she started work at a laundry shop close to home and was also working in her brother Gus's live poultry shop.

In 1955 or 1956, she traveled to Ft. Lauderdale, Florida, for her cousin Mike James's wedding. When she saw the palm trees, the sandy beaches, and the ocean, she decided then and there to leave Pittsburgh with its dreary winters and coal dust polluted air from the steel mills. At that time, Pittsburgh was the capital steel city of the United States. Today, the steel mills are gone and the city has become clean.

Upon her return from Florida, Alice sold her sewing machine and, with some money her mother had given her, said good-bye to her family and friends and headed for Florida, where she has resided ever since.

Her first years in Miami were filled with fun and adventures. She shared an apartment with some girlfriends in Miami Beach and danced away the nights at the Boom Boom Room of the Fontainebleau Hotel.

Alice met Jack Sweet, a handsome university student eight years her junior and fell in love. They married and had their first son, Christopher, in 1964. Two years later, Alice gave birth to a second son, Paul.

Alice's first marriage ended in 1969. Jack Sweet had returned from Vietnam, where he had served as an Army lieutenant, a changed man, as did most of the servicemen who fought in the war.

This is when I entered her life. In December 1969, I was on my way to visit my sisters in Hawaii when I stopped in Miami to see my Marine Academy friend captain Panos Giannakos. My friend was employed on the *M/V Freeport* (M/V stands for motor vessel, a ship powered with a diesel engine for its propulsion), a cruise ship sailing from Miami to Freeport in the Bahamas.

Waiting in the port of Miami for the *M/V Freeport* to be docked, a Greek who was also waiting to meet some friends informed me that the Greek community of Miami was having a dance at the Miami Shores Country Club. He invited me to attend.

Panos and I spent time reminiscing about our years in the Marine Academy as well as the time we served together on the same ship,

I as chief engineer and he as captain. We parted when the *M/V Freeport* sailed for the Bahamas.

In Miami for a few more days, I found myself with the keys to a car my friend had given me to use for my stay. I drove to Miami Shores Country Club to attend the dance. I was sitting alone at a table when two ladies and an elderly white-haired man approached and asked if they could join me. It was Alice, her father (Chris Stambolis), and Alice's friend Ida May. Around midnight, Alice, Ida and I took Alice's father home, and the three of us went to IHOP for breakfast.

After dropping off Ida, I took Alice home but parked there until around three o'clock in the morning, enjoying her hot lips. I have found them delicious ever since.

The next day, I went fishing and caught many fish. I drove to Alice's home and instead of flowers I presented myself with a large pizza-size platter full of fresh fish. Her father, a big fish lover like most Greeks, welcomed the fish, but not so much the fisherman. He was still hoping that his daughter would somehow reconcile with the father of his grandchildren.

I stayed in Miami for a while, and then I flew to Hawaii to visit my sisters Voula and Anna. Voula's husband, an officer of the United States Army, was serving in Vietnam, and Voula had moved to Hawaii with her three children, James, Louis, and Georgia. I had sent my sister Anna (who was still unmarried) to keep Voula company and help with the kids.

Chapter 3

My Seafaring Years

On the morning of August 19, 1959, I kissed my mother, sisters, and brother Tassos (Louis was studying engineering at the polytechnic university in Rome, Italy) and accompanied by my father to downtown Athens, where we boarded the train for Piraeus. Piraeus is the port city for Athens.

At the harbor, my father was apprehensive and emotional, anticipating the departure of his youngest son not only from the family's nest, but from Greece as well. Although my father and I had contradictory ideas, there was still a strong bond between us.

I was calm and ready to venture into the world and meet the challenges of a seafaring life. When the time for embarkation arrived, I gave my father a hug and kissed his hand in respect as was then the custom in Greece. I promised to be careful and write as often as possible. Once aboard the passenger vessel *Aitolia*, I waved to my father at the dock and gradually saw the skyline of Piraeus disappear in the afternoon mist. My seafaring years had begun.

The port of Piraeus, Greece

My destination was the city of Port Said in Egypt, where I had to meet and board the tanker the *North Prince*. I had signed a contract with its owners, Papadakis Maritime Company, to serve as apprentice engineer for a year. My first salary was sixty British pounds per month.

Aitolia's port of call was the city of Alexandria in Egypt, where I had to catch a train to Port Said.

Aitolia's route from Piraeus, Greece, to Alexandria, Egypt

The Mediterranean Sea was calm, and the trip to Alexandria was very smooth. On the *Aitolia,* I shared a cabin with five more passengers—British, Germans, and Americans. Also on the ship I met another graduate from my academy, an apprentice captain who was going to Alexandria to join a Greek cargo vessel for his apprenticeship. On the morning of August 21, 1959, the *Aitolia* approached the port city of Alexandria founded by Alexander the Great in 331 BC, whose fame was known to me not only from history and geography, but from the writings of the Greek poet Constantine Cavafis, who was born in Alexandria and had immortalized the city in his work.

As the *Aitolia* entered the port of Alexandria around seven in the morning, I was on deck anxious to see the famed city of Cavafis. The view was true to Cavafis's poetic description. Also, it reminded me of Cavafis's poem "Ithaca," appropriate for my sentiments at the time (Ithaca, the island of Odysseus or Ulysses).

Ithaka
As you set out for Ithaka hope your road is a long one,
full of adventure, full of discovery.
Laistrygonians, Cyclops, angry Poseidon—don't be
afraid of them: you'll never find things like that on your
way as long as you keep your thoughts raised high,
as long as a rare excitement stirs your spirit and your
body.
Laistrygonians, Cyclops, wild Poseidon—you won't
encounter them unless you bring them along inside
your soul, unless your soul sets them up in front of you.
Hope your road is a long one.
May there be many summer mornings when, with what
pleasure, what joy, you enter harbors you're seeing
for the first time; may you stop at Phoenician trading
stations to buy fine things, mother of pearl and coral,
amber and ebony, sensual perfume of every kind— as
many sensual perfumes as you can; and may you visit
many Egyptian cities to learn and go on learning from
their scholars.
Keep Ithaka always in your mind.

Arriving there is what you're destined for.
But don't hurry the journey at all.
Better if it lasts for years, so you're old by the time you
reach the island, wealthy with all you've gained on the
way, not expecting Ithaka to make you rich.
Ithaka gave you the marvelous journey.
Without her you wouldn't have set out.
She has nothing left to give you now.
And if you find her poor, Ithaka won't have fooled you.
Wise as you will have become, so full of experience, you'll
have understood by then what these Ithacans mean.

*

Years later in 1990, I would take Alice and our daughter Georgia
to Ithaca, the island of Ulysses, to visit the site where the old seafarer
had returned after twenty years from his departure for Troy.

Ulysses's island Ithaca

Alexandria was the site of one of the seven wonders of the ancient
world, the famous Lighthouse of Alexandria. Even greater than the
lighthouse was the library of Alexandria, which had accumulated

manuscripts with the knowledge and literature of the ancient world. Unfortunately, the library was burned down by Christian fanatics who also murdered Hypatia, the last curator of the library.

The murder of Hypatia (she was skinned alive)

A magnificent modern library has been built today at the ancient site.

The Lighthouse of Alexandria   Alexandria and the modern library

At the port of Alexandria, an agent for Papadakis Maritime Company met me and took me to the train station bound for Port Said. On the trip, I was fascinated to see for the first time the landscape of Egypt with its palm trees, banana plantations, date trees, and villages with homes or adobes made out of earthen blocks resembling termite mounts. I also saw live camels for the first time.

Earthen adobes   Camels along the canal

The train from Alexandria arrived in the city of Benha for a stop. Here I witnessed pandemonium when hundreds of Egyptians tried to board the train by pushing, shoving each other, and apparently arguing in their Arabic language. A man succeeded in lifting his children, wife, and their baggage through a window. When the train started to move, he also climbed through the window, leaving behind an old lady (maybe the mother-in-law) who was screaming and yelling. The incident was hilarious.

On the second part of the train trip to Port Said, I experienced another phenomenon. As the train cruised along, the sky darkened with clouds of sand. The windows were closed and soon the cabins became very hot. Outside there was no visibility at all, and despite the closed windows, the sand entered the train's cabins, making breathing difficult. Everybody in the train had to cover their mouths and nostrils with a handkerchief. It was something I had seen only in the movies—a sand storm.

Finally, the train arrived at Port Said, and an agent took me to a hotel where I stayed until the tanker *North Prince* arrived.

Port Said is a very interesting city with colonial architecture and colorful bazaars and other sights. While waiting for my ship to arrive, the agent showed me Port Said's night life. I liked the belly dancers, who were the best I had seen.

Port Said is located on the Mediterranean Sea and was built at the entrance to the Suez Canal, which was opened in 1869. The man-made canal connects the Mediterranean Sea and the Red Sea. Before its construction, ships had to navigate around Africa to call on ports in the Far East.

There is an interesting connection between the history of Port Said and New York. When the French sculptor Auguste Bartholdi sculpted the statue known today as the Statue of Liberty, it was designed to be installed in Port Said and represent the light of Egypt. The authorities in Egypt thought the project was too expensive, and the statue was finally brought to New York Harbor where it famously stands today.

The Statue of Liberty

On August 22, 1959, my first ship, the tanker *North Prince*, arrived at the anchorage of Port Said. At four thirty in the afternoon,

I boarded the *North Prince* and presented myself to the captain, giving him a package I had brought from the Piraeus office.

The tanker *North Prince*

After the captain, I presented myself to the chief engineer and handed over the letter of introduction from the manager of the Papadakis Maritime Company. The chief engineer was a German who was very pleased to get an apprentice engineer with higher education and could speak some English.

Although still an apprentice engineer, I was given a cabin in the officer's deck and assigned to dine with the ship's officers. This was an exception from the old custom, where all the apprentices were in the crew accommodations.

The *North Prince* entered the Suez Canal and thus I started my first professional voyage. August is a very hot month in Greece, but what I experienced aboard the *North Prince* in Egypt was a new kind of heat. Although I had my own cabin, the ship, like all the ships at that time, had no air-conditioning system. At night when I went to sleep, the heat was close to 100 degrees Fahrenheit. Even with the porthole open and the door of the cabin partially open, the cabin was like an oven. When I tried to sleep on my side, sweat filled my ear, and I had to change sides. Soon the other ear filled with sweat, and this went on until morning when I had to start work. *Well*, I said to myself, *I chose seafaring, and I have to learn to cope with these conditions.*

In my cabin aboard the tanker *North Prince*

While the heat was unbearable in the Suez Canal, I was about to experience even more severe hot weather when the *North Prince* entered the Red Sea. The ship was headed to the Persian Gulf and the port of Mena Al Ahmadi in Kuwait, which principally is an oil port.

The *North Prince* specialized in the transportation of crude oil from the oil fields to the refineries. The ship was powered by a MAN diesel engine of 7,500 HP for its propulsion, and it had three auxiliary diesel generators for its electrical needs. I was assigned to stand watch from twelve to four at midday and midnight. In the engine room, or rather the boiler room, which was connected to the main engine room, there were two boilers for steam.

As the ship cruised the calm waters of the Red Sea, the Arabic peninsula was at its portside (the nautical term for left side) and at its starboard (right side) was the northeast part of Africa.

I spent my free time on deck with my portable radio listening to Arabic music, which to me was new and very exotic. The Arabic music brought to my mind the stories of *Arabian Nights, The Adventures of Ali Baba and the Forty Thieves,* and of course, *Sinbad the Sailor.* These were movies I had seen and loved. One of the books I had brought with me from Greece was *Sand and Foam* by Khalil Gibran, a poet, philosopher, and artist who was born in the Mediterranean country of Lebanon. In particular, I liked two quotes. The first was:

> *I am forever walking upon these shores,*
> *Betwixt the sand and the foam,*
> *The high tide will erase my foot-prints,*
> *And the wind will blow away the foam.*
> *But the sea and the shore will remain Forever.*

Khalil Gibran was not aware that there is no forever. Today, we know that our life-giving sun eventually will run out of energy and become a white dwarf, and our Earth will cease to exist. Nevertheless, I liked the poetic expression.

The second quote from Khalil Gibran, which became a compass for my morality, was:

> *Seven times have I despised my soul:*
> *The first time when I saw her being meek that she might attain height.*
> *The second time when I saw her limping before the crippled.*
> *The third time when she was given to choose between the hard and the easy, and she chose the easy.*
> *The fourth time when she committed a wrong, and comforted herself that others also commit wrong.*
> *The fifth time when she forbore for weakness, and attributed her patience to strength.*
> *The sixth time when she despised the ugliness of a face, and knew not that it was one of her own masks.*
> *And the seventh time when she sang a song of praise, and deemed it a virtue.*

I think everyone should study this quote and try to give it his or her own interpretation. "Soul" for me is not what most religions accept as an entity that survives the death of a person. To me, "soul" is the "mind." "Mind" is the state of our brains. When the brain is dead, so is the mind with all the data accumulated there in a person's lifetime.

In the 1950s, radio was the only entertainment for mariners. The *North Prince* and all the ships in that era communicated with the home port of Piraeus and the ports of call through radio. A radio officer was on watch to receive or send messages by the wireless station of the ship. When the ship was far from land, the communication was done using Morse code. Of course this is obsolete today because of the modern satellite communications with sound and pictures.

When the *North Prince* entered the Persian Gulf, the temperatures in the engine and boiler rooms climbed to 110 to 120 degrees Fahrenheit. On the platform on top of the engine, where I had to go and check the temperatures of the cylinders, it was 140 to 145 degrees. The engine and boiler rooms were ventilated by electric fans, some sending fresh air and some removing the hot air (exhaust). Standing under the air vents provided some relief, but in the August heat of the Persian Gulf, the supplied air was still hot. The crew of the tanker was instructed to drink plenty of water or other liquids, and the captain distributed salt tablets to be taken daily to replenish the lost salt from the constant perspiration.

From the Red Sea, the *North Prince* entered the Gulf of Aden and then the Arabian Sea, which is the north part of the Indian Ocean. Here I had my first whale sighting. A pod (group of whales) of the magnificent mammals was only a few miles from the ship. Excitedly, I ran on the bridge to get binoculars and stood in awe as I watched the whales up close, breathing through their blowholes and frolicking on the surface of the ocean. The ship continued on its course to the Gulf of Oman, past the Strait of Hormuz, and entered the Persian Gulf.

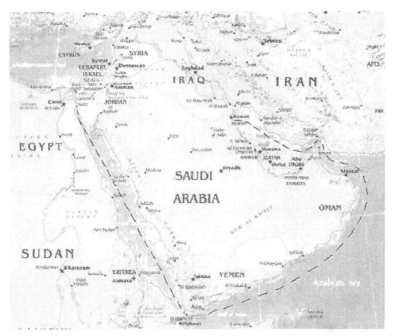

My first voyage from Port Said, Egypt, to Mena Al Ahmadi, Kuwait

On the morning of September 4, 1959, the *North Prince* arrived around seven in the port of Mena Al Ahmadi, where the tanker was loaded with crude oil for Europe. I visited the seamen's club, and for the first time I met Arab people.

In the town, the majority of Arab men wore a long-sleeved one-piece dress that covered the whole body, called a *dishdashah* or *thoub*. This garment allows the air to circulate, which helps cool the body during the hot summer days. The dishdashah is usually made of white cotton to reflect sunlight. With the dishdashah, men also wear a three-piece head cover. The bottom piece of this head covering is a white cap that is sometimes filled with holes. This cap, called *thagiyah*, is used to hold the hair in place. On top of the thagiyah is a scarf-like head cover that comes in two types: a light, white head cover called *gutrah*, which is worn during summer, and a heavy red and white checked head cover called a *shumag*, which is worn during winter. These head covers protect the head and face from direct sunlight and can be used to cover the mouth and the nose during sand storms or cold weather. On top of the thagiyah and the gutrah is the *ogal*, which is a black band surrounding the top of the head to hold everything else in place.

What astonished me was the way women in Kuwait were dressed. They wore a long-sleeved, loose, floor-length dress called an *abaya*, which is a silky head-to-toe black cloak. Their faces were covered by a scarf and veil that allowed only their eyes to be seen. I was not only learning about the machinery and operation of ships, but I was getting an education studying the local cultures of the places my ships were taking me.

On September 5, 1959, the *North Prince* left the docks of Mena Al Ahmadi loaded with crude oil and bound for the port of Ravenna in Italy.

Back through the Persian Gulf, Indian Ocean, Red Sea, and the Suez Canal, the tanker entered the Mediterranean Sea and headed for Italy. New countries, new cities, and new cultures kept me busy learning, studying, and expanding my knowledge both in my engineering profession and my understanding of the various peoples and their countries that, until then, I knew about only from books.

I stayed on the *North Prince* from August 22, 1959 to October 18, 1960. During the thirteen months and twenty-seven days aboard the tanker, I went back to Kuwait, Iraq, and Iran in the Persian Gulf and Syria in the Mediterranean Sea to load with crude oil, and again returned to Europe to deliver it to various ports. I had the chance to visit England, France, Germany, Belgium, and Italy while employed on the *North Prince*.

On January 26, 1960, the *North Prince* left the port of Hamburg in Germany and headed back toward the Persian Gulf. When she was close to Gibraltar, the radio operator received new orders. The ship was instructed to cross the Atlantic and head to Venezuela. Winter in the North Atlantic is very treacherous, but when I heard the new destination, I was pleased with the prospect of visiting a new continent and crossing the Atlantic Ocean.

The captain, who had experienced the North Atlantic, charted the new course from Gibraltar south to the Azores Islands and from there west to the northeast part of South America and Venezuela. On February 13, 1960, after eighteen days at sea, the *North Prince* arrived at the port of Maracaibo.

Venezuela and South America was a new experience for me. The people, the music, the colors, and the language were fascinating. I visited Maracaibo and learned some of Venezuela's history.

On right in Venezuela with another crew member

An interesting incident took place when I and some other fellow crew members tried to take photos in front of the statue of Simon Bolivar (Bolívar [July 24, 1783-December 17, 1830] was a Venezuelan political leader credited with contributing decisively to the independence of the present day countries of Venezuela, Colombia, Equator, Peru, and Bolivia. He is revered by all those nations as a national hero). We were approached by angry Venezuelans who threatened us. I tried to tell them that we were Greek crew members, and we also considered Simon Bolivar a hero. The incident ended with friendly remarks and apologies.

On February 14, 1960, the *North Prince*, loaded with crude oil from the huge oil field of Esso in Maracaibo, left Venezuela for the Isle of Grain in England, which is a large refinery facility east of London. We crossed the Atlantic once again, through the Azores and then along the coasts of Europe to England. It was my first transatlantic voyage. Over the next ten years, I would plow the Atlantic many times on other ships to call on the United States and Canada, passing through the Panama Canal south to Peru and north to Alaska.

My time on the *M/T North Prince* was interesting and adventurous. My free time was spent reading the books I had brought with me from Greece as well as those I found in the ship's library. Another activity that took my attention was watching the stars on clear nights; from the deck I could study the constellations. Sky-gazing is better on the open sea where there are no other lights to interfere.

I was fascinated with the sea both when she was calm and when the waves pounded the ship. When the tanker was loaded, the deck was covered with foaming water. We experienced the heaviest seas at the Bay of Biscay off the coasts of Spain and France, where the sea can be very treacherous.

Experiencing the tempest of the wild sea

In winter, the Mediterranean Sea was also rough, and when the tanker was loaded, the cook would pick many flying fish from the deck where they had landed accidentally. Many birds would also land on the ship for a rest on their migration from Europe to Africa.

Relaxing on the deck   Up on the mast

Conditions on the *M/T North Prince* while in the hot regions of the Red Sea and the Persian Gulf were very uncomfortable, especially working down in the engine and boiler rooms. On my last trip to the Persian Gulf, I became dehydrated and lost too much salt despite drinking plenty of liquids and taking salt tablets. As a consequence, I became ill with pains in all my joints and severe headaches. My chief engineer, Mr. Hartman, relieved me from all of my duties, and I remained in my cabin for several days resting and drinking lots of fluids. Finally, I regained my health. After this experience, I vowed not to seek employment again on tankers.

When the *North Prince* returned from the Persian Gulf, I disembarked in the port of Ravena in Italy still weak from my ordeal and thus ended my first employment with the Papadakis Maritime Company.

In Ravenna, Italy

On the *M/T North Prince* I became good friends with the third engineer with whom I started my watch duties. His name was Nikos Rouvas. We have remained friends for life. When I returned to Greece, I visited Nikos's family in Athens and became the godfather to his daughter Katerina.

With goddaughter Katerina

With Katerina in Greece (1990)

Although an atheist, I took my role and duties as godfather very seriously. I have kept in touch with the Rouvas family and my goddaughter Katerina to this day. In 1982, now married to Alice and living in Miami, I brought Katerina for a visit to meet our daughter Georgia and our two sons, Christopher and Paul. Alice and I visit with the Rouvas family whenever we travel to Greece.

With my friend Nikos Rouvas (2007)

From Ravenna, I went to Rome where my brother Louis studied and my oldest sister Voula lived. I stayed with them for several days before returning to Greece. Louis and Voula took me around Rome and the vicinity to visit all the archeological sites and points of interest.

With Louis and Voula in Rome (1961)

Years later (1990), our daughter Georgia graduated from Miami Country Day High School. As a present, we took her on a six-week tour of Europe to visit many countries and cities, including Rome.

Alice and Georgia at Meteora, Greece Venice, Italy (St. Mark's Square)

Amsterdam   Paris (Montmartre)

The Acropolis in Greece   Venice, Italy

Today, after centuries of hate and animosity, the countries of Europe cooperate with each other and coexist as one European Union, eliminating all borders and establishing the Euro as their common currency.

After my stay in Rome with Louis and Voula, I returned to Greece. Having completed the required sea service as apprentice, I registered for the examinations to obtain my third engineer's license. I passed the exams and officially became a third engineer for vessels with diesel engines of any capacity.

With Louis studying in Rome, two sisters still living at home, and my oldest brother Tassos also living with the family and not working, finances were difficult since my father Dimitrios had retired from the army.

Even on my first maritime employment when my salary was small, I helped with Louis's expenses. With my upgraded license, I was eager to go back to sea and take over the responsibility for Louis's education in Rome. On December 24, 1960, a day before my name day celebration, I again said my good-byes to family and friends and left Greece to join the freighter *M/V Dona Katerina* in Hamburg, Germany.

The Dona Katerina

My new ship, although smaller than the *North Prince*, flew the Greek flag with Piraeus as its registered port. Like most Greek freighters, the *Dona Katerina* operated as a tramp vessel. That means she was not trading on a regular line, but after each voyage, she would receive her orders for the next port of call.

As third engineer on the *Dona Katerina*, I earned a salary of $300 per month, and the company paid the premium dues to the Greek seamen's retirement fund (similar to Social Security in the United States). This enabled me to take over my brother's tuition and living expenses in Rome.

Another big difference on a tramp ship was the amount of time she stayed in port for loading or unloading. On a tanker, the loading or unloading of crude oil took no more than two to three days, but a tramp freighter with general cargo such as the *Dona Katerina* stood in port for several more days. Many times, the docks were occupied with other vessels, and she would have to wait at anchor for days. The anchorage places were usually outside the harbors, and the crew would be allowed to visit the city with a boat provided by the ship's agent.

The anchorage was usually an excellent place for fishing. I and other members of the crew spent our free time at this activity.

What I liked most on the new ship was the opportunity to see and explore the various ports and nearby cities, visiting their museums and places of interest. I also enjoyed interacting with the local people, especially girls!

The *M/V Dona Katerina* traded between ports in Europe for a while, but then she was loaded with scrap metal from Amsterdam with its destination Tokyo, Japan. The trip from Europe to Japan was the longest at sea for me—forty-eight days.

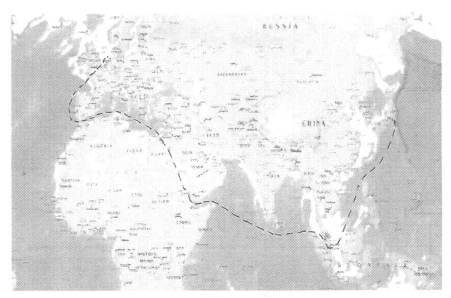

My longest trip of forty-eight days at sea
(Amsterdam, Holland to Tokyo, Japan)

From Amsterdam, the *Dona Katerina* passed the English Channel to the Atlantic Ocean. Entering the Straits of Gibraltar into the Mediterranean Sea, the heavily loaded ship crossed the Suez Canal and entered the Red Sea. At the port of Aden in Yemen, she stopped for provisions and some engine maintenance repairs. Yemen is a small country on the southwestern side of the Arabian Peninsula.

The crew was advised not to visit the town of Aden because there was some kind of revolution going on and safety for foreigners was uncertain. I was of course disappointed. Departing Aden, The *M/V Dona Katerina* entered the Arabian Sea and the Indian Ocean heading for the southern tip of India and the Island of Sri Lanka, which at that time was called Ceylon, the world renowned island of spices and tea.

When the ship was close to India, I listened to the music from this mysterious country of mystics, which I had read about in books and seen in the movies. I hoped one day seafaring would bring me to India, the country of Mohandas Karamchand Gandhi, Rudyard Kipling, and Rabindranath Tagore.

Tagore and Gandhi

Kipling

To me, Gandhi was the inspiration for pacifism and peace, and Rudyard Kipling's poem "If" was another source of guidance. Years later I gave my daughter Georgia and her husband Derek a framed copy of the poem on one of their wedding anniversaries. It is still hanging in their bedroom.

If

If you can keep your head when all about you
Are losing theirs and blaming it on you;
If you can trust yourself when all men doubt you,
But make allowance for their doubting too;
If you can wait and not be tired by waiting,
Or, being lied about, don't deal in lies,
Or, being hated, don't give way to hating,
And yet don't look too good, nor talk too wise;
If you can dream—and not make dreams your master;
If you can think—and not make thoughts your aim;
If you can meet with triumph and disaster
And treat those two imposters just the same;
If you can bear to hear the truth you've spoken
Twisted by knaves to make a trap for fools,
Or watch the things you gave your life to broken,
And stoop and build 'em up with wornout tools;
If you can make one heap of all your winnings

And risk it on one turn of pitch-and-toss,
And lose, and start again at your beginnings
And never breath a word about your loss;
If you can force your heart and nerve and sinew
To serve your turn long after they are gone,
And so hold on when there is nothing in you
Except the Will which says to them: "Hold on";
If you can talk with crowds and keep your virtue,
Or walk with kings—nor lose the common touch;
If neither foes nor loving friends can hurt you;
If all men count with you, but none too much;
If you can fill the unforgiving minute
With sixty seconds' worth of distance run—
Yours is the Earth and everything that's in it,
And—which is more—you'll be a Man my son!

Thinking of my granddaughter Ella, I edited the last line to read:

"And—which is more—you'll be a proud person my child!"

Rabindranath Tagore, the other Indian thinker I had read about and admired, was a contemporary of Gandhi. He was a poet, author, philosopher, and, most of all, he was an advocate of universal education. Like me, he was convinced that humankind would advance only through education. Rabindranath Tagore founded a school in his birth place of Santiniketan, which later became a university known today as one of the best in the world. Tagore was awarded the Nobel Prize in 1913 and contributed the money to his school.

The *Dona Katerina* passed Sri Lanka and proceeded to the Malaca Strait with Malaysia on her portside and Indonesia on her starboard. Crossing the Singapore Strait, she entered the China Sea to her final destination of Tokyo, Japan. I had read Nikos Kazantzakis's travel book *Japan* and was anxious to see the country and meet its people. Traveling along the coasts of the islands of Japan, I was impressed with their landscape and green foliage. Finally, the ship docked at the unloading site, and I was able to step ashore for the first time to a Far East country.

In Japan

The *Dona Katerina* stayed in Japan several days, and I had the chance to visit and explore the capital of this fascinating country. In Tokyo, I visited the many interesting sights, museums, and the famous Ginza district with the phantasmagoric shops, cafes, bars, and cabarets. I also went to some beautiful parks with pagodas and the replica of the Eiffel Tower, which was constructed in 1958 as a telecommunications tower. The view of the immense city from the observation deck of the tower was breathtaking. I found the Japanese people very agreeable and happy in spite of their terrible losses during World War II.

In front of a pagoda.

From Japan, my ship sailed to Australia to be loaded with wheat, which was stored in the cargo holds in bulk.

In Australia

Again, I was thrilled with the prospect of exploring a new continent and a new country. In Australia, the *Dona Katerina* called at Perth in southwestern Australia and Sydney and Melbourne in New South Wales. I wanted to meet the surviving aborigines of Australia that, like the American Indians, had been hunted and practically eliminated. I got my chance years later when I went to Australia with another ship.

At Perth, Sydney, and Melbourne, I met many Greeks from the flourishing Greek communities there, and I was surprised to bump into a fellow Greek with whom I had served on the destroyer *Glory* in the Greek Royal Navy. Like most of the Greeks, he offered me warm hospitality, taking me to his Sydney home and family, where I met his lovely wife and infant boy.

From Australia, my ship with general cargo was sent to New Zealand, which I found very beautiful and the Maori girls very charming. Back to Australia, the *Dona Katerina* was loaded with wheat for China, destination: Qingdao, a major port city of mainland China.

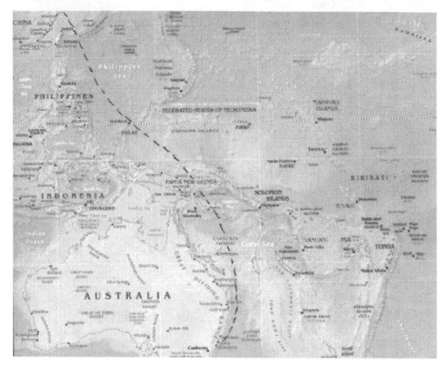

From Sydney, Australia to Qingdao, China

China was another country I had wanted to visit. I had read the adventures of Marco Polo and the stories of how monks smuggled the silkworms hidden in the hollow of their walking sticks. At that time, China was the only country producing silk, and the penalty for smuggling the precious silkworm eggs was death. I was also fascinated with China's civilization, the oldest in humankind's history, and her philosophers, namely Confucius and Lao Tse.

Born in 551 BC, Confucius was a great thinker. He emphasized that a person's status should be determined by his or her ability instead of ancestry, wealth, or religious dogmatism and affiliation, as is unfortunately the case in America today as well as most other countries in the world.

I had also read Nikos Kazantzakis's travel book on China and the masterpiece novel *The Good Earth* (translated in Greek) by the American author Pearl S. Buck, who was born in China. Pearl Buck is one of my favorite and most admired writers. All of her books are in my library. I admired Lao Tse, the other Chinese philosopher, because he advocated that we should "act without acting" by saying and doing what is genuinely felt rather than putting on a show for others.

Qingdao, which is also known as Tsingtao, was the birthplace of Lao Tse and also where the world famous Tsingtao Brewery is located. When Alice and I go to a Chinese restaurant, I always have Tsingtao beer.

When the *Dona Katerina* arrived in Tsingtao, China was still under the rule of communism and Mao Tse-Tung, the communist leader. Mao is regarded as one of the most influential figures in modern world history. In the 1960s, the insanity of the Cold War permeated the planet, and China was very suspicious of foreigners.

While the *Dona Katerina* was at anchor waiting for the pilot to arrive, a launch with a group of Chinese officials boarded the ship and ordered all hands on deck. They examined all the passports and finally gave their approval to enter into the harbor.

I and the crew of the *Dona Katerina* stayed in Tsingtao for several days. Unfortunately, we were not allowed to visit the city on our own. The local government provided us with tours escorted by armed guards. Among other places, they took us to a theater to see a play with the actors dressed in colorful costumes and painted masks. Watching the pantomimes on the stage, I figured that the play was extolling the communist revolution in China. I found the music and the singing very monotonous, but we all remained stoically to the end.

The *Dona Katerina* remained in the Far East, and during her voyages in the Yellow Sea, I experienced my first typhoon. Our ship was returning to Australia empty, and for five days we were battered by nature's fury. Sleepless and exhausted, we managed to escape sinking and listening to the radio reports of other vessels close by that were not so lucky. Three other freighters sunk, one of them of Greek registry.

I was employed on the *Dona Katerina* from December 24, 1960 to July 2, 1961. I disembarked in Sydney, Australia, and took a Greek cruise ship as a passenger for my return to Greece to do my military service. The long cruise from Sydney to Athens was very enjoyable for me, as I met a lovely young Dutch girl who was returning with her family to Holland.

On the cruise ship *Australis*

In Piraeus, we said our good-byes, and I returned to Athens and my family. Louis and Voula were in Athens as well, so the whole family was reunited. With me in Greece for two-and-a-half years for my service in the Royal Navy (Greece was still a kingdom), finances for the family became difficult again. My ever-dynamic mother Georgia had already started a small business a few years earlier. She had sold the orange grove in Amykles, and with the proceeds bought an apartment in downtown Athens that she rented for extra income. Then she built an addition to our house at Papagos and opened a grocery store.

My mother Georgia with Tassos at the grocery store

On a hot Sunday, August, 13 1961, my two brothers and I, our mother and father were having lunch when my father complained of chest pains. Voula and Anna had gone to the beach a few miles from Athens.

We consulted a neighbor, a retired army doctor, who advised us to take my father to the military hospital in Athens. We called a taxi and with me in the front and my father between Louis and Tassos in the back, we sped toward Athens and the hospital. By the time we reached the emergency room, our father was unconscious. The doctors tried everything, but to no avail. Around three that afternoon, our father was pronounced dead.

Although I was the youngest of the three brothers, I took charge of the situation. Relatives and friends were informed, and a funeral with military honors took place three days later.

I entered the Royal Navy training camp on October 2, 1961. Many of my classmates from the Marine Academy were at the camp, easing the insanity of the training as well as my state of mind after the loss of my father. I despised the stupidity of military training (daily marches, crawling and jumping over obstacles, and most of all the brainwashing by narrow-minded instructors who emphasized God and country).

After four months and six days of basic training, we were given an oath to defend the country, the Greek flag, the king, and the Greek religion. I, along with all the draftees, raised my hand with the three fingers joined together, representing the father (God), the son (Jesus), and the Holy Spirit of the Greek Orthodox religion, which I considered primitive and ludicrous, and took the oath. (To do otherwise, I could have faced court-martial.).

Years later, I said to my grandson and granddaughter, "You should never forget that where sanity ends, the military and religious minds begin."

If members of any armed forces today paused to think that individual soldiers have no quarrel with soldiers of the opposing army, that they too have families and loved ones, that the orders for most wars come from individuals who don't only participate in it but instead act for personal or ideological gain, then perhaps the atrocity of war would be curtailed.

In sailor's uniform with Voula   Giving the oath, I am the fourth from left

After basic training, I received the rank of commissioned officer and was ordered to report for duty on the destroyer ΔΟΞΑ (*Glory*), where I served the rest of my Royal Navy days.

As commissioned officer of the Greek Royal Navy

On the destroyer, I served twenty-five months and fourteen days. I was in charge of one of the two engine rooms of the ship, and I was also responsible for the operations of the destroyer's engineering office. The "lost years," as I characterized them, came to an end on March 22, 1964, when I was discharged.

Free now from military service, I was eager to resume my professional seafaring vocation. On April 20, 1964, I traveled by train to Hamburg, Germany, to join the *M/V George M Embiricos*, my next cargo vessel, as third engineer.

In front of the *M/V George M Embiricos*

My new ship was a beautiful cargo vessel with good accommodations and an engine room with a Sulzer diesel propulsion engine. On the ship I was pleasantly surprised to meet Nikos Manouselis, a classmate from high school in Athens and also my classmate at the Marine Academy.

Nikos Manouselis left and me on the *M/V George M Embiricos*

Nikos Manouselis and I had been drafted at the same time in the Royal Greek Navy, but we served on different navy ships.

Me at left, Bill Tzavaras center, and Nick Manouselis right, Marine Academy classmates at the Greek Navy training camp.

Our service together on the *M/V George M Embiricos* brought us closer, and we have remained good friends ever since. Years later, when I stayed permanently in Florida and married Alice, I learned that my friend Nikos had also abandoned seafaring and was married and living in Chicago, Illinois. We resumed our friendship, communicating by phone or mail.

From Nikos, I learned that two more classmates from the Marine Academy, George Karazanos and George Spyrakopoulos, had also abandoned their merchant marine carriers. George Karazanos, like Nikos, ended up in Chicago working for International Harvester, and George Spyrakopoulos immigrated to Winnipeg, Canada. We all four classmates still exchange phone calls, greeting cards, and photos of our families.

When I joined the crew of the cargo vessel *M/V George M Embiricos*, she was trading in North Europe. From Hamburg, Germany, Nikos and I traveled with our ship to London, Southampton, and Liverpool in England, Glasgow in Scotland, and Dublin and Belfast in Ireland. It was the era of the famous musical group The Beatles. I loved their music and especially John Lennon's song "Imagine," whose lyrics I would mention later in my atheist speeches and writings.

In Liverpool, Nick Manouselis and I, along with some others from the crew, went to the Cavern Club where the Beatles became famous.

In London I visited the museums and places of interest, including the British Museum, where the largest collection of sculptures and other artifacts from ancient Greece was housed. It was stolen by the Earl of Elgin, who allegedly had obtained a controversial permission from the Ottoman authorities to remove pieces from the Acropolis in Athens. Greece was then occupied by the Turks and part of the Ottoman Empire.

Nick Manouselis, a deck officer, and I went to Greenwich to see the famous National Maritime Museum, the clipper Cutty Sark, and the Greenwich Observatory, where the imaginary meridian divides the globe into east and west. Naturally, we spent some time and money in Soho, the red-light district of London.

Nick Manouselis
left,third captain,center
and electrician G.
Vandoros at Greenwich

At Buckingham Palace

In 1981, when our daughter Georgia was nine, Alice and I took her to London and visited the British Museum and the other interesting places that I knew from my travels.

Greenwich

Buckingham Palace

In front of Big Ben

Museum of Natural History

Cutty Sark

In the Museum of Natural History

From Europe, the *M/V George M Embiricos* was loaded with general cargo destined for the United States. She crossed the North

Atlantic, which at that time was rather calm, and entered New York Harbor and the Hudson River, heading toward her final destination, the capital of New York State, Albany. As the ship entered New York Harbor, I saw the Statue of Liberty on the ship's port side and the island of Manhattan with its skyscrapers on her starboard side.

I wanted very much to visit the city of New York, not only to see the famous Empire State Building and the other sights, but to meet the many relatives from both my mother's and father's sides who had immigrated there. New York was also the place where my mother Georgia had lived with her three brothers and sister in the early 1900s. However, the *M/V George M Embiricos* proceeded toward Albany, and I would have to wait a few more years before visiting the Big Apple.

From Albany, the *M/V George M Embiricos* traveled to Canada to the city of Churchill. I had never experienced cold weather like that of this frozen arctic region. Conditions were so brutal that when we had to do repairs or maintenance work on the ship's steam operated winches on the deck, we couldn't stay exposed to the elements for more than ten minutes. By then our fingers wouldn't be able to close and hold a tool.

Finally, the *George M Embiricos* set her course for the Panama Canal and the Pacific Ocean. Cruising through the Caribbean Sea, I marveled at the hundreds of dolphins playfully racing against the ship at her bow and the many flying fish darting through the dark blue waters of the Caribbean. Before entering the Panama Canal, our ship docked at the port of Cristobal, the city at the entrance of the canal on the Atlantic side. Nikos and I went ashore to see the city and its colorful inhabitants.

Passing through the Panama Canal for the first time, it was a thrill to see this marvel of engineering. Since the sea levels between the Atlantic and Pacific Oceans are different, the ships passing through the canal have to be lifted and then lowered.

Our ship entered the first locks called the Miraflores and when the gates closed, the lock was filled with water, lifting the ship. From the Atlantic locks, we entered Lake Gatun and took about ten to twelve hours to cross the forty-eight miles to reach the Pacific. There we again entered the locks to bring the *George M Embiricos* to the Pacific sea level. There is a difference of about eighty-five feet between Pacific and Atlantic.

In the Pacific, the *George M Embiricos* set course north for Port Hueneme, which is south of the city of Los Angeles in California.

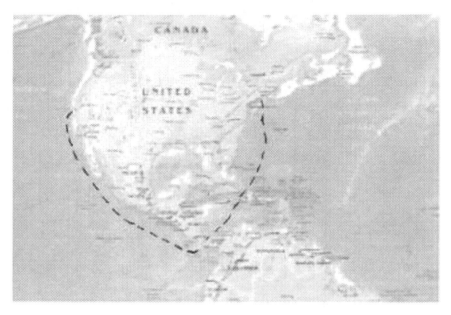

From Albany, New York, to Port Hueneme in Los Angeles, California

Now twenty-six years old, I went ashore with Nick at Port Hueneme and stopped at a dancing place and bar. The proprietor of the bar thought that I was under twenty-one, the age allowed entrance. I had to produce my ID to be allowed to enter the bar. The experience was new to me because in my native country of Greece there were no such restrictions.

Port Hueneme in Los Angeles, California

It is ironic that US law forbids young people to have a glass of beer or wine, but at eighteen it is acceptable to be sent to war and kill other people! I said later to my grandchildren, "You might hear a song written and performed by a favorite artist and activist of mine, Pete Seeger (Joe Hickerson wrote some of the verses)."

The title of the song is "Where Have All the Flowers Gone."

Where have all the soldiers gone, long time ago?
Where have all the soldiers gone?
Gone to graveyards, everyone.
Oh, when will they ever learn?

From Port Hueneme, our ship got its orders to go north to British Columbia on the Pacific side of Canada. We arrived in the picturesque city of Victoria, which is one of the most beautiful cities my travels have taken me. After Victoria, the *George M Embiricos* went further north, passing through some breathtaking scenery along the coast of British Columbia to Prince Rupert. The landscape of all of British Columbia was a profusion of indescribable verdant beauty. When Nick and I went out walking through the forest, we saw many wild animals, among them deer and some enormous moose.

From a nearby pulp mill on Watson Island, the ship was partially loaded with paper rolls, and from the same area we received baseball bats as well as aluminum ingots.

While our ship was docked in Prince Rupert, a group of Greeks from the Greek community there noticed the Greek flag of the ship and came to meet their compatriots. They invited us to visit their community. They also had their own soccer team, who challenged the crew of our ship for a game or match, as they called it. Remembering my soccer years from the academy, I and the other young crew members formed a soccer team.

Naturally, we lost the game, but we had a very enjoyable day. I had not played soccer since my academy days, and I was very sore the next day.

Fully loaded, the *George M Embiricos* left beautiful British Columbia and entered the North Pacific destined for Japan. The Pacific Ocean, true to its name, was dead calm, but when the ship was a few miles off the coast of British Columbia, she entered into a foggy area with zero visibility. It was a new experience for me—when I went up to the ship's bridge, I couldn't see her bow. It was an eerie feeling. The captain ordered the fog horn to be on a timer, and two sailors were ordered to stand at the stern and bow of the ship periodically knocking a gong-like instrument. Foggy conditions in the North Pacific can be dangerous and last for days. It reminded me of Edgar Allan Poe's book *The Narrative of Arthur Gordon Pym of Nantucket*, which I had read in my youth. This mysterious adventure had fascinated me and ignited my imagination. However, the story was set not in the Pacific, but in Tristan Da Cunha, a remote volcanic group of islands in the South Atlantic Ocean.

Eventually we passed the foggy region of the North Pacific, paralleled the Aleutian Islands, and after a smooth voyage arrived at the northern and second largest island of Japan, Hokkaido.

The capital of Hokkaido is Sapporo, where in 1972 Japan hosted the first Winter Olympic Games ever held in Asia. My friend Nick Manouselis and I explored this island with its quaint villages, pastoral countryside of rice paddies, pagodas, and gardens of exquisite beauty. We also met two girls, Mico and Kyoko. They were university students from Tokyo on a break visiting their families.

Me, Nick, and Miko standing; Kyoko, the chief
engineer, and a third mate sitting.

When Miko and Kyoko heard that our ship was going to
Tokyo, they invited us to visit their place in a suburb of Tokyo.
After the cargo for Hokkaido was unloaded, she sailed south to
Tokyo. I had already visited Tokyo when I was with the freighter
Dona Katerina.

In Tokyo, Nick and I boarded a train that took more than an
hour to arrive at our friends' station. By then it was evening, and
using the address on a paper written in English and Japanese,
we found the girls' small house and rang the bell. Waiting for
some time, we realized that neither the girls nor any other
occupants of the house were there yet. We decided to explore the
neighborhood, which was typically Japanese. There were single
homes with gardens, and the streets were like alleys. Nearby we
found a place that seemed to be a bar and went inside to inquire
about Miko and Kyoko. Unfortunately, nobody spoke English,
but from the paper with the address and the names, the locals
pointed at the clock, trying to tell us to wait for Miko and Kyoko
to come home.

The Japanese offered us drinks, and when an old man with white
hair and beard heard the name of Greece that I had mentioned
when trying to tell them our nationality, he got excited and started

hopping up and down, arms waving and shouting, *"Girisha, Girisha,"* which meant "Greece, Greece." He started naming the Greek philosophers he knew, like Socrates, Plato, and others. I wanted to know more about this old scholar, but it was impossible. Neither spoke the other's language.

Later on, after finding the note I had left at her door, Miko came to get us. Our adventure in that part of Tokyo left fond memories for Nikos and me.

From Japan, the *George M Embiricos* returned again to Europe, where a new apprentice engineer joined the ship. To my and Nick's surprise, the new apprentice was from the academy and had just graduated. When I was a senior, Apostolos Tsergas was a sophomore, and we had been good friends.

Me (on the right) and Apostolos Tsergas on the *M/V George M Embiricos*

Nick and I guided and taught the new apprentice all we knew from our experiences at sea. On June 29, 1965, Nick Manouselis and I disembarked together from the *George M Embiricos* in Hamburg,

Germany, and returned to Athens by train. I had been on the ship a total of one year, two months, and ten days.

On our train trip from Hamburg to Athens, Nick and I had two adventures worth mentioning. The first took place in Italy, where we had to change trains. At the station in Milan, we unloaded our suitcases. We also helped the captain's wife, who had disembarked the ship and was returning to Greece with us. When the new train arrived, I carried some of her suitcases into the cabin and was ready to return to the platform where Nick and our suitcases were. From the window of the cabin, I saw a well-dressed Italian man take Nick's suitcase and proceed toward the exit. I hollered at Nick, who hadn't noticed that the thief had taken his suitcase. Nick Manouselis is from Sfakia, a mountainous region of Crete. The Sfakians were once great sailors and even greater pirates, but they were always great warriors who played a leading part in all the struggles for freedom in Crete. Even today they remain fine specimens of Cretan manhood. Once realizing the attempted theft, Nick charged after the Italian who, seeing the ferocious Cretan, abandoned the suitcase and ran for dear life.

The second incident took place when the train was in the former Yugoslavia. Nick and I were having lunch in the dining car when the train entered the station at Belgrade, the capital of Yugoslavia, and stopped. We and some other passengers remained in the dining car, expecting the train to continue on to Athens. After some time had passed, we realized that the dining car had been disconnected from the main train, which had already departed for Greece. Our complaint to the authorities that no public announcement had been made was to no avail. We were stranded in Belgrade until the next train for Athens arrived twenty-four hours later.

Fortunately, I had my passport and money with me, but Nick had left his at the compartment with the captain's wife. After a while, a young and very attractive girl was sent to assist us. She spoke very good English and arranged for us to spend the night in a hotel.

We sent a telegram to Thessaloniki, the next stop of the train, requesting that our luggage be left there. The incident ended the next day when we boarded the train for Greece and Thessaloniki, where we found our luggage.

In Athens, Nick and I parted ways and didn't see each other until years later. In 1974, when I was married and living in Miami, Florida, I took Alice, sons Chris (eight years old) Paul (seven) and daughter Georgia (two) on a trip by car to Canada. On our way, we stopped in Chicago where Nick lived, and we met again, introduced our families, and talked of the years that had passed.

Back in Greece, I had now the required sea service to upgrade my license from third engineer to second engineer. I applied for the exams, and on December 15, 1965, obtained my second engineer certificate #1213 for vessels of any capacity with diesel engines.

I stayed in Athens until February 1966. When my savings began to run low, I contacted some maritime companies and was hired as second engineer by Fafalios Maritime Company to serve on their freighter the *M/V Stamos*. On February 7, 1966, I flew to London where I joined the *Stamos* as its second engineer. The owners of the ship were from the island of Chios, whose inhabitants are seafarers and shipowners. They are also religious and superstitious. The *Stamos* was at the port of Amsterdam in Holland when a Greek priest came aboard to bless the vessel and its crew. I was in the engine room when the priest opened the door and stood on the platform to perform his mumbo jumbo religious ritual. To the horror of some crew members, I chased him out of the engine room, telling him to take his superstition elsewhere. A witness to the priest's expulsion told the rest of the crew what happened, and they all felt that a disaster would befall their ship because of the infidel second engineer. They were afraid the ship would sink.

With the *Stamos* loaded, we left Amsterdam with orders to cross the Atlantic, pass through the Panama Canal to the Pacific Ocean and proceed south to the port of Callao in Lima, the capital of Peru.

Crossing the Atlantic, we met some heavy seas, and the crew was more petrified than ever, blaming me, the infidel, for their imminent demise. To top off their fears, in the middle of a strong gale one night, the auxiliary generator broke down, and the ship was immersed in a blackout.

With flashlight in hand, I went down to the engine room and assisted the third engineer on watch to start the other auxiliary engine and, to crew's relief, restored electricity to the ship. I had to work hard during the next few days under adverse conditions, but by the time the ship entered the calmer seas of the Caribbean, I had completed the repairs, and the ship was again seaworthy.

Beyond the Panama Canal, we turned south, parallel to the coast of South America, toward Peru and Callao. Along the eastern coast of South America off the coasts of Ecuador and Peru, there is a current that plays a very important role in the climate not only of the region, but the whole of North America as well. I had learned in the academy of the various ocean currents, but the experience of entering the El Nino was startling. The ocean brimmed with millions of fish as thick as soup. To my astonishment, the *Stamos* plowed right through this sea of fish.

We arrived in Callao, where we stayed for several days unloading our general cargo. I had time to visit Lima and take an excursion to the ancient ruins of Cusco, which is high on the Andes Mountains. Cusco was the capital of the Inca Empire. The Incas had a remarkable civilization long before the Spaniards invaded their empire, captured Atahualpa, the last Inca emperor, slaughtered thousands of Incas, and plundered their treasures of gold and precious stones.

The story of Atahualpa is a monumental example of the horrors of the Catholic Church, the Spaniards, under their leader Francisco Pizarro, and the priests who went along to "Christianize" the Incas. Pizarro and the Catholic priests of the Holy Inquisition condemned Atahualpa to be burned at the stake as a heretic because he had refused to accept their Christian religion. When he was told that he would be burned at the stake, afraid his soul would not enter the next life in accordance with Inca belief, he accepted the offer to be baptized for a lenient sentence. The Catholic priest commuted the sentence to death by strangulation or *garrote*, as is the Spanish term. It is a barbarous practice of execution in which the victim dies a slow death.

Years later, when I was married to Alice in Miami, I met Mr. Papadopoulos, a Greek businessman from Lima who invited me and Alice to visit Peru as his guests. We accepted the offer and flew to Peru with our daughter Georgia, who was only an infant. It was in the spring of 1973.

Mr. Papadopoulos, who owned two hotels in Lima, gave us his seaside condo furnished with a maid, a limousine, and a chauffeur to take us around. We had a very enjoyable time. When Alice and I returned to Miami with our daughter, I helped Mr. Papadopoulos find and purchase a hotel in downtown Miami. We remained good friends until Mr. Papadopoulos's sudden death at seventy-nine a few years later.

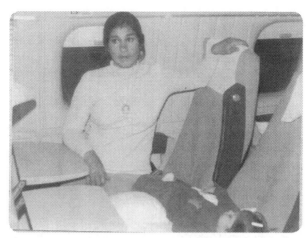

Alice and daughter Georgia on the plane to Peru

With the *Stamos* now empty, we left Callao and went north on the coast of Peru to the port of Chimbote to load with fishmeal for Amsterdam. I learned that the fishmeal used for animal feed came from the millions of fish our ship encountered on our way to Peru. The sardine-sized fish are processed in ovens and pulverized into its final form of fishmeal. The fishmeal is stored in the open in huge mounds similar to salt mounds I had seen in Greece.

When I asked the locals about rain, I was informed that the coast of Peru, when the El Nino is normal, never receives any rain. The high mountains of the Andes retain all the moisture and rains that feeds the rivers (including the Amazon jungles) of the Andes and the vast rainforests east in Brazil. The Amazon is the biggest river in the world and flows through the rainforest of Brazil to the Atlantic side of South America. During the rainy season, parts of the Amazon exceed 120 miles in width, and because of its vast dimensions, it is called The River Sea.

The *Stamos* remained in the port of Chimbote for several days to load the fishmeal with its characteristic fishy smell. In fact, the smell permeated the whole city and the surrounding countryside. When other members of the crew and I went ashore in Chimbote, the chicken we ate at the local restaurants had the fishmeal smell and taste. Apparently, all the livestock in Chimbote were fed with fishmeal.

In Chimbote, some other officers of the *Stamos* and I rented a car and drove to the city of Trujillo, north of Chimbote, not only to escape the smell of fishmeal for a while but to explore the coast of Peru and see the archeological sites that the ship's agent suggested. I enjoyed the beautiful city of Trujillo with its many plazas and buildings from Spanish colonial times, as well as the largest pre-Columbian city of Chan Chan, about five kilometers from Trujillo. Today Chan Chan is considered a World Heritage site.

The ruins of Chan Chan

When we returned to Chimbote, the ship, fully loaded with fishmeal, left the smelly port for the long voyage back to Europe and Amsterdam.

The voyage north to the Panama Canal and into the Caribbean and the Atlantic was uneventful until one day I happened to stop at the ship's galley, where the cook was ready to cook some meat. What repelled me was the cook's filthy apron. I reprimanded the cook, and then upon entering the galley, I noticed that the meat he was ready to place in a pot was practically rotten and unfit for human consumption. Infuriated, I grabbed the container with the meat and tossed everything overboard.

Of course the incident was reported to the captain, who called me to his office. To my surprise, the captain, an old-timer, attempted to pacify me by offering to instruct the cook and the ship's steward to prepare anything I wanted as long as I refrained from further interferences. The bribery made me angrier yet, and I gave the old captain a lecture on the new rules and guidelines contained in the Greek Maritime Union contract that I always carried with me.

The *Stamos* arrived in Amsterdam, and the crew was happy and now more sympathetic with me despite my nonreligious ideas. The ship stayed in port for several days not only to unload, but also because of a strike of the longshoremen of the port.

I found myself free of duties for a while and decided to visit my sister Voula, who was with her family in Stuttgart, Germany. My mother and younger sister Anna were there as well. I boarded a train and left for Stuttgart for the weekend. When I returned to Amsterdam, I found there was a replacement for me. Since I had been fired, the company paid my first class fare back to Greece, giving me all the severance pay due to me by the law.

To my surprise, the crew of the engine room offered me presents in appreciation of what I had done for them. In addition to the food improvements that resulted from the disposal of the rotten meat, I had also demanded that the ship's steward provide fresh linen weekly as the Greek Seamen's Union contract prescribed. I had also given some talks on hygiene, especially the dangers of venereal diseases in the ports. Since most of the young seamen were shy, when in port, I would go to a pharmacy and get dozens of condoms for them. In those years, condoms were not available on the pharmacy shelves. You had to ask a clerk. If the clerk was a woman, the shy sailors would not ask for them.

I was truly moved by the appreciation of these good-hearted seamen and sincerely thanked them. I served on the *Stamos* from February 7, 1966 to July 11, 1966, for a total of five months and three days. This was my shortest sea employment.

With extra money in my pocket, I returned to Stuttgart where I surprised my mother and sisters and spent some more time with them. From Stuttgart, my mother, Anna, and I returned by train to Greece, where I spent an extra vacation until my next seafaring employment.

On October 23, 1966, I was employed on the M/V Κυρα Ελενη *(Lady Helen),* a beautiful small freighter owned by the widow of an executive of the legendary Aristotle Sokratis Onassis and one of his lawyers. From Athens, I traveled by car to the port of Pilos at the southwestern Peloponnesus. The *Lady Helen* was on her route to Turkey to load animal feed, a byproduct of cotton. The seeds of cotton are processed to form flat pies, a very nutritious feed for cows and other animals. The *Lady Helen* was scheduled to pass off Pilos, and I had to be transported by boat to meet her on the open sea and board her.

By the time I made it aboard the *Lady Helen,* it was midnight. The next day, when I met the third engineers and the engine room crew, I detected a chilly attitude. Apparently, the second engineer that I replaced was fired for some reason, and they thought that I was a company's man. I put on a coverall, a flashlight in my pocket, got a pad and pencil, and went down to the engine room. As I had done with all the other ships, I traced all the piping systems of the ship, and in no time I knew the ship like the palm of my hand.

Soon after, the atmosphere changed, and officers and crew became very friendly with the very young-looking second engineer. I was twenty-eight years old, a very young second engineer by Greek standards.

The freighter *M/V Lady Helen*

The *Lady Helen* was my last ship under Greek ownership and one of the best in my seafaring career. On May 7, 1967, the chief engineer left the ship while she was in Venice, Italy, and the company appointed me to take his place. Although I had only my second engineer's license, I accepted the position and became the chief engineer of the *Lady Helen*.

The *Lady Helen* was built in Trondheim, Norway. The engine room was converted later from steam engine to diesel. Removing the boilers and steam engines made the engine room of the *Lady Helen* very roomy and one of the best in which to work. I loved the *Lady Helen* not only because it was my first ship as chief engineer, but because with her I visited many countries including Italy, France, Belgium, Germany, Poland, Norway, Sweden, Finland, and Denmark in Europe, Turkey and the Soviet Union on the Black Sea, and Morocco, Tunisia, and Libya in North Africa.

As chief engineer on the *Lady Helen,* I had more free time to do more reading, which was my favorite pastime. To improve my English, I read many books in the language. With an English-Greek dictionary, I labored for many hours while on the open seas. I was always convinced that "reading is to the mind what exercise is to the body."

On November 27, 1967, when the *Lady Helen* called in Venice, Italy, I disembarked to return to Greece. From Venice I boarded a train to Brindisi, a port city in the Adriatic Sea, and from there I embarked on a ferry boat that took me to Patras in Greece. From the port of Patras in the northwest of the Peloponnese, I again took a train for Athens and home.

I served on the *Lady Helen* one year, one month, and four days. I have warm memories of my time spent on her. In Poland, I had met a very sweet girl with whom I corresponded by mail and phone. Unfortunately, I lost the letters from Ewa in a burglary, as well as other papers I had kept in my warehouse in Miami.

Ewa

Ewa and me (Poland)

Another funny anecdote from my time spent on the *Lady Helen* took place in Trondheim, Norway. The captain and I were invited to a party by the ship's agent. The weather in Norway was very cold, so I put on a suit but underneath I wore several more garments and my pajama bottoms to keep warm. On top, I wore my heavy overcoat, scarf, gloves, and hat. When we left the ship, I felt fine. A taxi took us into town to the building where the party had already started. We entered and gave our overcoats, scarfs, gloves, and hats to the clerk and proceeded to the main dancing hall. The place was heated, and most of the ladies were dressed in gowns, some of them even sleeveless. Pretty soon I started to feel very uncomfortable. My body got hotter and hotter and my face more and more red. I excused myself and went to the bathroom where I took the excess clothing off, including the pajamas. I hid the bundle of the discarded clothing behind a trash container with the intention of getting them back later. From then on, I felt better, and the rest of the evening was very pleasant. When the party was over, I escorted one of the ladies to her home and forgot the hidden clothing. It was a small price to pay.

Back in Greece, having completed the required service, I applied for the examination to the ministry of the Greek Merchant Marine and on April 12, 1968, received my chief engineer's license #1056. I was twenty-nine years old with license to serve on any vessel powered by diesel engines of any capacity.

My chief engineer's certificate

Although I was a qualified chief engineer, I decided to remain ashore after both good experiences and bad circumstances such as typhoons, gales, and stormy seas. I invented a new hanger for men's trousers for which I obtained a patent from the Greek Ministry of Commerce.

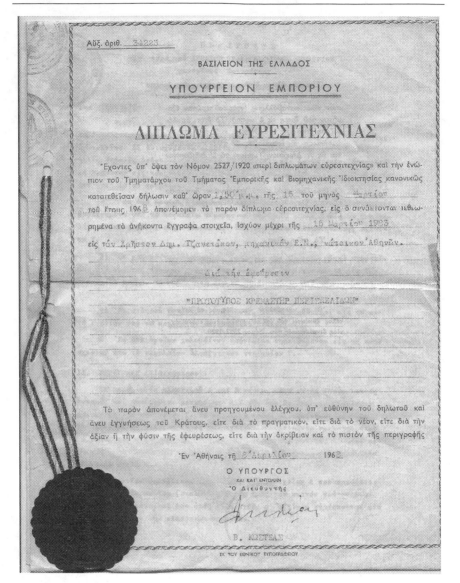

My Greek patent certificate

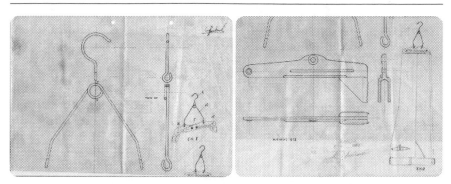

The drawings of my Greek patent

Using my engineering skills, I built the tools necessary for the production of the spring and the hanging hook of the hanger. I commissioned a mold-maker to make the mold and a plastic company to produce the parts. When all the parts were ready, my mother, brothers, and sister Anna became the first workers in my new enterprise. The whole operation of assembling the hangers was carried out in the apartment where my family lived in Athens.

The assembled hangers were placed in boxes and carried out to a small warehouse I had rented. The neighbors in the condominium were curious to know what was coming in and out of the apartment, but my family and I kept the operation secret because manufacturing in the apartment was against the condo rules.

I hired a young woman as salesperson who started successfully selling the hangers door-to-door to shops and enterprises that, at that time, were mostly owned by men. She was pretty and had long, shapely legs she emphasized with short skirts. Greek men were compelled to buy a few hangers even if they did not need them. I even exported some of my hangers to the United States.

A businessman now, I was making money, and the young saleswoman was making a fortune as well until two things happened. First, the fashion of bell-bottomed pants was introduced, and my hangers were unfit for the wider pants. Second, I got tired of the Greek bureaucracy with its many regulations.

Alice with my hanger (I kept one hanger for my records)

Then in October 1968, my friend Captain Panos Giannakos, who I knew from my academy years, called and asked me to join as chief engineer on the mother ship for a fleet of fishing vessels. The fleet was part of Gulf Fisheries Co., a company owned by Sheik Sabah of Kuwait.

With my friend Panos Giannakos (right)

Gulf Fisheries had over a hundred modern fishing boats equipped with Caterpillar and Rolls Royce engines. The fleet was fishing for shrimp in the very rich waters of the Persian Gulf. It had four mother ships where all the shrimp catches were taken for processing, packaging, and storage in their refrigerated holds.

When Captain Panos Giannakos contacted me in Athens, he was the captain of the mother ship *M/V Failaka 20* and fleet captain for twenty-one fishing boats and a smaller mother ship that had left Kuwait and the Persian Gulf and sailed to Indonesia to explore the waters there for new fishing grounds.

I accepted the offer to be the chief engineer on the *Failaka 20* and fleet engineer for the fishing boats and the second mother ship the *M/V Dasman 10*.

Since I was going to be responsible for the entire fleet, I negotiated a salary of $900 per month, a salary that was almost double the amount paid to chief engineers on Greek ships at the time. The company accepted, and in addition to the salary, they offered me a bonus for each ton of shrimp netted by the fleet.

So my seafaring years started again, and I had to leave Greece for more sea adventures. Of interest here is the name of the *Failaka 20*. Failaka is an island in Kuwait that, in the third century BC, was colonized by Alexander the Great. It was renamed Ikaria because its shape resembled the Greek island of Ikaria in the Aegean Sea.

My friend and I boarded a plane for the long flight to Indonesia to join the fleet. We arrived in Medan, a port city on the island of Sumatra. Indonesia was a new experience for me. I had read of the pirates in the region in its past history, and especially of the Malaysians just north of Sumatra.

The fleet waited for Captain Giannakos and me to take it from Medan to the Malaysian island of Penang, where it would undergo some general repairs for the next expedition in search of new fishing grounds. The next day after their arrival in Sumatra, I was still asleep in my cabin when I was awakened by gunshots and shouts. I thought for sure pirates were attacking the ship. However, it turned out that a group of Indonesian soldiers with their officer had boarded the ship and demanded to see Captain Giannakos. The fleet had an agreement to stay in Sumatra for a year, but not finding satisfactory fishing grounds, had notified the authorities of their decision to depart from their waters. After some tense negotiations, Captain Giannakos gave the officer cigarettes and money, and the fleet was allowed to sail for Penang.

I thought that it was a close call with the angry and ferocious-looking Indonesians, but all ended well, and we sailed from Medan to Malaysia.

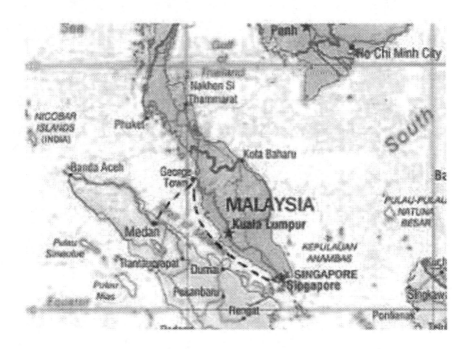

From Medan to Penang (George Town) and then
Penang to Singapore

It was the beginning of my adventure in the Far East, an adventure I remember fondly and was indirectly responsible for me coming later to America where I met Alice.

I visited all the vessels and talked with their crews. They were an international group. The captains of the fishing vessels were Mexican and Greek, with crews from Sudan, Palestine, Jordan, and other Middle Eastern and African countries. On the *Failaka 20*, the officers and crew were also international, including a German refrigeration engineer, Poles, Palestinians, Americans, British, a Turk, and of course, the captain and I both Greeks. Communication was in English, which was tolerably understood among us.

The fleet stayed in Penang for about a month and Captain Giannakos and I had a wonderful time. Every evening we would go out to Penang and visit the Tiger Bar where we met some local girls. Another of our favorite places was the rooftop of the biggest hotel in town, where there was a restaurant and bar with a dancing stage and an orchestra. We became regular customers, and whenever we entered, the orchestra would play the Greek song "The Children of Piraeus," known internationally from the movie *Never on Sunday*.

I was fascinated with the small, beautiful island. I rented a car and for a few hours explored its sights from one end to the other. At a remote place I stopped at what seemed to be a temple or shrine. The temple was dedicated to snakes, and I agreed to be photographed holding the snakes in my hands and placed around my neck. (Other tourists had done the same before me.) Later I found out that the snakes were poisonous, and the authorities had cautioned the tourists of their danger. Thankfully I was not harmed.

With poisonous snakes in Penang, Malaysia

With the girls from the Tiger Bar at the beach in Penang

With Elizabeth (a Eurasian girl) in Penang

The fun time in Penang ended when all the repairs were completed and the fleet sailed from Penang to Singapore, where we were going to take on provisions for the next expedition for fishing grounds in Papua New Guinea, north of Australia. With sadness, my friend Panos and I had to say our good-byes to Penang. It had been a happy and adventure-filled place for the two of us. The short trip from Penang was smooth. All the fishing boats and the two mother ships entered the straits of Singapore safely. They were docked and ready to receive supplies for the longer voyage to Papua New Guinea.

I liked Singapore with its British colonial buildings and shops that reminded me of London. What I did not like was the news from the home office of Gulf Fisheries in Kuwait. Captain

Panos Giannakos was fired from his position. As I learned later, the reason for my friend's termination was that he allowed women aboard the *Failaka 20* and also purchased beer and other alcoholic beverages, which of course was against strict Muslim standards of Gulf Fisheries.

My position was spared because the company couldn't find a replacement, and perhaps the Muslim crew members of the engine room, with whom I had developed a very good relationship, sent a good report about me.

My friend accepted his termination and flew back to Greece. He searched for new employment and found a position on the cruise ship *M/V Freeport I* sailing from Miami to Freeport in the Bahamas Islands.

A year later, on my way to Hawaii to visit my sisters, I stopped in Miami, Florida, to see my friend on the *Freeport*, thus staging my future decision to come to the United States.

The only Greek now on the *Failaka 20,* I prepared the fleet for the long voyage from Singapore to Port Moresby in Papua New Guinea.

From Singapore to Port Moresby, Papua New Guinea

The convoy of the twenty-one fishing trawlers and the two mother ships left Singapore, entered the Java Sea with Borneo to the port side and the chain of the Indonesian Islands to the starboard side, paralleled Timor Island, and then entered the Arafura Sea. In the Arafura Sea, the fleet, with the western part of the Indonesian New Guinea Island to their port (New Guinea is divided into western Indonesia and east, or Papua New Guinea), and the Gulf of Carpentaria to the starboard, entered Torres Strait to the Coral Sea and the Papua Gulf for the final stretch to Port Moresby, the capital city of Papua New Guinea. It was Christmas when the fleet entered the port of Port Moresby, and the authorities along with the media gave us glorious welcome.

In 1968, New Guinea was one of the few spots on the planet not yet fully explored. The eastern part of New Guinea was under the protectorate of Australia as Papua New Guinea. When the fleet arrived, there were rumors that several missionaries were killed and eaten by cannibal tribes in the interior highlands of the island. In the early 1960s, I had read the newspaper reports about Michael Rockefeller, the son of American billionaire Nelson Rockefeller. Michael Rockefeller disappeared, and his body was never found. Like the missionaries, it believed that he was killed and eaten by cannibals.

The fishing fleet was welcomed to Papua New Guinea not only for bringing business to the local economy, but because the Gulf Fisheries Company had agreed to employ a percentage of the fleet's crew with native Papua New Guineans. I was sad to see all the Chinese from Singapore who were hired when the fleet was in Indonesia replaced by Papuans. The Chinese were smart and very good mechanics. Most of the Papuans had no experience with engines, and their employment in the fishing fleet as assistants in the engine rooms was disastrous.

Port Moresby became the base for the new fishing expedition, and I became fascinated with the opportunity to explore the island close to Port Moresby and the primitive Papuans. Like Michael Rockefeller, I wanted to study these people, whose very rich island was being invaded by foreigners from all parts of the world greedy to extract as much gold, copper, oil, and timber from their soil as they could.

The island was also invaded by a horde of missionaries from all religions and denominations who wanted to save the souls of these children of nature. Until the advent of the insane religious notion of sex as sin and the shame of nakedness, they were very happy in their primitive societies and culture. As with the American Indians, the Eskimos, the Aborigines of Australia, and other native peoples around the globe, they were introduced to white man's alcohol and other diseases. The missionaries did the greatest job in grabbing the best land and subjugating the Papuans with the fear of hell and eternal damnation. It was the same scenario as in Kenya where Jomo Kenyatta stated:

> When the missionaries arrived, the Africans had the land and the Missionaries had the Bible. They taught how to pray with our eyes closed. When we opened them, they had the land and we had the Bible.

I loved Papua New Guinea and the happy natives around Port Moresby. With my second engineer, Yousef Saleh Diab, who was one of my best staff members and a good friend, we often drove into the nearby village of Boroko, bringing with us bags of candy and small presents for the village kids. Seeing the two of us approach, teenage boys and girls would swarm to meet us the village square. The boys would bring their guitars, and everyone would sing and dance for us. Unfortunately they were already contaminated by the missionaries. They were taught to wear clothing not to protect their bodies from the elements, but to please the Christian god of the missionaries who told them that nakedness was a sin.

Another interesting native event was the gathering of many tribes or villages at an open field outside of Port Moresby for a special occasion. They called these gatherings "sing sing," and they could last many days. The natives, dressed in their traditional costumes of feathers, masks, and painted bodies, would feast on roasted pigs and fruits along with a very potent alcoholic drink made from fermented roots. Yousef and I would go to these gatherings and even taste the food and drinks offered by the Papuans.

The fishing fleet remained in Papua New Guinea more than six months. The mother ship *Failaka 20* was in port most of the time, while the rest of the fishing trawlers and the smaller mother ship the *Dasman 10* were out searching the waters of the Papua Gulf.

The operation for the Gulf Fisheries Company of Kuwait was not getting favorable reports, and finally the fleet was ordered to return to Kuwait. During the fishing expedition to Papua New Guinea, I inadvertently became part of what was an environmental crime. Fishing with long nets to sweep the bottom of the sea, the trawlers caught thousands of fish, snakes, sea turtles, and seashells with their living occupants, along with the desired shrimp. When the catch was brought on the mothers ships, the shrimp were separated and the rest, mostly dead by then, was thrown back into the sea. Even the great tiger sharks or smaller members of their species were victims of the fishing nets.

Holding the fin of a great tiger shark, a victim of the fishing nets

The departure from Port Moresby and Papua New Guinea was very sad for me. During our over six month stay there, I had met a native girl from Manus Island who was studying in Port Moresby to become a nurse. Her name was Rachel Bondokey. Rachel was the happiest and most genuine girl I had ever met.

She was a child of nature (she was still in her teen years), free with her emotions, always with a sweet smile, unpretentious, and without any ulterior motives for her love for me. The day of the fleet's departure and our final separation was cloudy, and my state of mind was heavy and gloomy. Seeing Rachel, with whom I had spent so many happy days and adventures, crying uncontrollably and clinging to me was heartbreaking.

With Rachel on the *Failaka 20*

The fleet left the waters of Papua New Guinea for the long voyage back to Kuwait. We once again passed the Torres Strait to Arafura Sea on route to Singapore, our first scheduled stopover.

In Singapore, I received letters from Rachel that again aroused my emotions. They were simply written, conveying her feelings and her state of mind in a way only a child of nature can do. As I read Rachel's letters, a lieutenant of the Australian Royal Navy whom the company had hired for the trip to Kuwait asked to see them. After reading them, he said that he had never before read more warm, sweet, and genuine letters. I cherished Rachel's letters and kept them with me. Unfortunately, they were lost years later in Miami when burglars broke into my warehouses and stole a box containing mementos from my seafaring life.

I never heard from Rachel again; my letters were not answered. Later, when I returned to Greece, I learned that an epidemic had struck New Guinea, leaving thousands dead. I assumed that the sweet girl of my Papua New Guinea romance, by then a nurse, had contracted the disease and died.

In Singapore we took provisions for the second leg of the voyage to Kuwait and set our course for the Indian Ocean. We passed the Malaca Strait with Sumatra now to our port and Malaysia to our starboard. In the Gulf of Bengal, the fleet set course for Sri Lanka.

Entering the Indian Ocean, the fleet turned north along the coast of India toward the Arabian Sea. Off the coast of India, we met some heavy seas, and two of the fishing boats lost their engines. The captain on the *Failaka 20* and the deck crew, fighting the great waves, succeeded in throwing towing lines and slowly resumed an altered course for Bombay, India, our new destination and refuge.

I welcomed the new destination, anxious to see Bombay and have a taste of India and its peoples. After some very anxious days of combating the Indian Ocean monsoons and the crushing waves, the fleet made it to Bombay, where we stayed several days until the bad weather subsided and the authorities allowed our departure. We also had time to work on the two disabled fishing trawlers and restore their engines for the final voyage to the home port of Kuwait.

I explored many of Bombay's sights. I encountered widely diverse social conditions, from the very rich and privileged with mansions and luxurious houses to the downtrodden poor living in tin-roof shacks in what I learned was the biggest slum in the world.

In 1969, the caste system was still very much alive despite the attempts of Gandhi to bring equality to the Indian population. I was happy to have an Indian aboard the *Failaka 20* whose family lived in a public housing project on the outskirts of Bombay. He invited me to meet his family, and I gladly accepted. I also asked to be taken around Bombay.

Slums of Bombay, India

Among the sights, he took me to the house where Gandhi stayed while in Bombay and also to the home of Rudyard Kipling.

The Kipling House, Bombay   The Gandhi House, Bombay

After a week or so in Bombay, the weather abated, and the fleet was now ready to resume its course to Kuwait. Leaving the sheltered harbor of Bombay, we set our course along the west coast of India toward the Arabian Sea. From there the fleet entered the Gulf of Oman, passed the Hormuz Strait, and reached the Persian Gulf, with the final destination of Kuwait ahead.

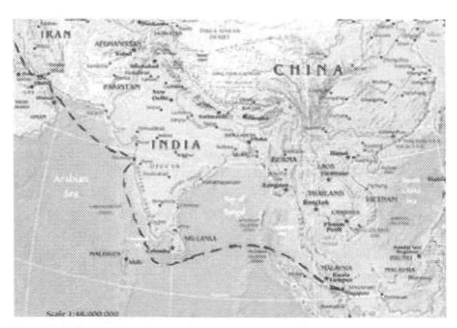

From Singapore to Bombay and Bombay to Kuwait

I was again in the Persian Gulf, where I had suffered from heat exhaustion and dehydration back in 1959 on the *M/V North Prince*. Of course, things were much easier now for me as chief engineer, but the heat and the social conditions in the strict Muslim country of Kuwait were not the ideal place for a freedom-loving person like me.

In Kuwait I met and befriended an older Greek gentleman who was originally from Thessaloniki, Greece, as well, and we found that we had mutual friends there. His name was Mr. Hatzigiannakis. He had moved to the region long ago with a friend and partner (Vlachos) with whom he had started an engineering company in Baghdad with branches in Kuwait, Saudi Arabia, and Tripoli in Libya. Mr. Hatzigiannakis introduced me to a minister of Kuwait, who offered me a permanent position in the communications ministry as chief engineer for their diesel emergency engines. This was a position with a generous salary and many benefits.

However, after working for a year with Gulf Fisheries, I had saved enough money and was anxious to return to Greece. I thanked my friends, and after exchanging part of my money for gold bullion that was plentiful in Kuwait, I left Gulf Fisheries and the hot Persian Gulf for Greece.

After one year and one month with the fleet of Gulf Fisheries, I returned home to Athens. It was November 1969.

I relaxed for a while, going to my beloved city of Salonika (Thessaloniki) to meet classmates and friends from my gymnasium years. I also visited with relatives in Amykles at Sparta, my father's hometown.

A few months before my return to Greece, I had sent money for my sister Anna's air ticket to Hawaii. My older sister, Voula Barclay, lived in Honolulu on the island of Oahu with her two sons and her small two-year-old daughter. Her husband Andrew, a United States army officer, was serving in Vietnam. I sent Anna to help Voula and keep her company. Just before Christmas, I decided to go to Hawaii myself and see the beautiful islands that captivated my distant relative George Lycurgos. Uncle George ventured to the Hawaiian Islands back in the 1800s and became a Hawaiian legend.

In Athens I learned that Elsa, a girlfriend from my academy years, was now a world-renowned soprano with the opera at Saint

Gallen in Switzerland. I called her, and she was very happy to hear from me. When I told her of my plans to fly to Hawaii, she invited me to stop in Switzerland. I flew to Zurich and from there drove to Saint Gallen, where I spent a few days. Elsa took me around and introduced me to her colleagues at the opera house. Switzerland in December was blanketed with snow, and the landscape around Saint Gallen was picture perfect.

With Elsa in Saint Gallen, Switzerland With Elsa's friend in Saint Gallen, Switzerland

Forty years later, in 2009, Alice and I met Elsa in Athens, Greece. I introduced Elsa to Alice, and we spent an evening at her Athens apartment. Elsa was a widow now living in Vienna, Austria, where she still taught music. In the summer she stayed in Greece. She gave us some of her CDs and an autographed photo from one of her opera performances.

Dedicated photo of Elsa Kastela
(To my childhood friend Christos and his Arete [Alice]
to remember me.)

I said good-bye to Elsa and her friends and continued on my trip. From Zurich I boarded a plane for Miami, Florida, where my friend Captain Panos Giannakos worked on the cruise ship *Freeport I*.

I was attracted to the thirty-four-year old Greek goddess with a million-dollar smile and a free and happy disposition. In addition, her shapely legs and perfect figure had smitten me like a school boy.

With Alice and her two sons, Paul left and Christopher
right in Miami (1970)

I stayed in Miami for a while, and then I flew to Hawaii to visit Voula, her three small children, James, Louis, and Georgia, and my sister Anna, promising Alice I would return to Miami.

I was also eager to visit the islands of Hawaii for another reason. When I was still a small boy growing up in Sparta, I had heard stories of a distant relative called Uncle George Lycurgus who became a legend in Hawaii when the islands were still an independent kingdom.

My childhood imagination was also aroused by the reading of pirate tales and stories of explorers of Africa and other parts of the world that were still unknown to my generation. The books of Jules Verne, Mark Twain, and other authors carried me to all the exotic lands that, eventually, my seafaring would bring to reality.

In all my previous seafaring years, my ships had never brought me to the Hawaiian shores, and now I found myself where Uncle George Lycurgus had become well-known and very successful. With my sister Voula, I flew from Honolulu of the Oahu island to Hilo, the capital of the big island of Hawaii, where I was told Uncle George had lived the last years of his long life. We met Uncle George's son Nicholas, who welcomed us to the Volcano House, a resort hotel on the rim of Kilauea crater. Nickolas Lycurgus was the manager of the Volcano House, and we had a very pleasant stay there. The Volcano House is now part of Hawaii National Park, but before its acquisition, it was owned by George Lycurgus and his brother Demosthenis.

Uncle George died in 1960 at the old age of 101 years. A book of his adventurous life has been written by Harry Miller Blickhahn, and a copy with a dedication was presented to me by Nickolas Lycurgus. The book is among the many books treasured in my library.

I enjoyed the Hawaiian Islands as much as Uncle George, although conditions were completely different since the islands became part of the United States.

Uncle George Lycurgus

After one month, because I had promised Alice I would return, I was anxious to go back to Miami and my Greek goddess.

Back in Miami, I met my friend Captain Panos Giannakos again, who introduced me to the management of the cruise ship *Freeport*. In addition to the *Freeport*, the company operated a container ship that sailed from Miami to Guatemala in Central America. They offered me a position on their container ship for one month and then a transfer to the *Freeport I*.

I accepted the offer and sailed on the container ship *CCT* from Miami to Puerto Barrios, the Caribbean port of Guatemala. In my short term on the *CCT*, I had the opportunity to visit the area close to Puerto Barrios. I was dismayed at the poverty of the Guatemalan people and the deplorable slums of the country.

The contrast of the haves and have-nots in Guatemala

After two or three trips to Guatemala, I was transferred to the cruise ship *Freeport I*, which became the last vessel of my seafaring career. Although a licensed chief engineer, I agreed to be second engineer on the *Freeport I* with a salary of $700 per month, which was more than the salary of chief engineers on Greek ships.

The *Freeport I* sailed from Miami every evening at six and arrived in Freeport, Bahamas at midnight. Then she departed from Freeport at six in the morning and arrived back in Miami at noon. This schedule was ideal for me as I was able to see Alice every day.

Time on the *Freeport I* was fun. I had less responsibility and the company encouraged the officers to mingle with the passengers when off-duty. I enjoyed dancing in the ship's ballrooms and other entertainment activities with passengers. I would bring Alice and her two small sons on the ship often while docked at the port of Miami and took them on many cruises with me to the Bahamas.

My relationship with Alice blossomed into love, friendship, companionship, and mutual respect that has lasted to this very day.

I never intended to remain in the States, but after several months into my relationship with Alice, I realized that she was the perfect mate for me.

In May 1970, I decided to apply for United States citizenship. I asked my brother-in-law, Captain Andrew Barclay, and Voula to sponsor me for the immigration papers.

AFFIDAVIT OF SUPPORT

We, Andrew and Paraskeve Barclay, being duly sworn, depose and state as follows:

1. That we are citizens of the United States of America, and that I, Andrew Barclay, am presently serving on active duty as a Captain in the United States Army at Fort Lee, Virginia.

2. That we shall support and accept full responsibility for all acts and debts incurred by Christos D. Tzanetakos and prevent him from becoming a public charge while he is in the United States with me between *May 15, 1971* and *until such time as he becomes a permanent resident.*

3. That this affidavit is submitted in support of application for visa for *the brother of Paraskeve, and the brother-in-law of Andrew.* IN WITNESS WHEREOF, I have hereunto set my hand the *11TH* day of the month of *MAY*, 1971.

Paraskeve G. Barclay
Andrew H. Barclay

ACKNOWLEDGEMENT

I, *R. STEVEN KROHN* the undersigned, do hereby certify that *Andrew & Paraskeve Barclay* whose names are signed to the foregoing affidavit of support, dated *May 11, 1971* has this day acknowledged the same before me in my jurisdiction aforesaid.

Given under my hand this *11th* day of the month of *May*, 1971.

R. Steven Krohn
Signature of officer with power of notary
U.S. Army, Ft Lee, Va

Because of my employment on the cruise ship and a bank account of several thousand dollars, the immigration officials approved my application. It was then that I found my other love besides Alice. Studying the history of the United States and its Constitution, I was enthralled to find out that the framers of the Constitution were mostly free thinkers of the European Enlightenment.

Having experienced the conditions of the police state in Greece and witnessing violations of individual human rights in other countries during my travels, I became a passionate and avid supporter of the Constitution and especially its First Amendment, which guarantees freedom of thought and expression.

Most of all, I appreciated the idea that the Constitution of the United States protects the rights of the individual. Five years later, on September 3, 1975, I became a United States citizen.

I worked on the cruise ship *Freeport I* until December 1970, which marked the end of my seafaring career as professional marine engineer. I disembarked in Miami and took some months off. I moved in with Alice and her two small boys, who accepted me as their new dad. To complete the family, Alice and I decided to have a child together. Wishing for a girl, we applied for marriage license and on February 4, 1972, we were married by a judge in the downtown Miami courthouse in a civil ceremony.

On December 13, 1972, our daughter Georgia was born and completed the family.

My seafaring years were over.

Chapter 4

Christos the Businessman

In 1971, when I decided to permanently stay ashore in Miami, I spent several months vacationing.

The year before when I was still working on the *M/V Freeport*, I had purchased a used Ford Mercury Meteor from the Greek who invited me to the dance at the Miami Shores Country Club in December 1969.

I paid $300. I realized later that I paid ten times more for the old car than I should have. Apparently the fellow Greek took advantage of my ignorance of the used car market. After I had paid the $300, I entered I-95 from downtown Miami to go to Alice's at Miami Shores. I had not traveled more than half a mile when the engine stalled. I checked the oil and found it was empty. *Well,* I thought, *it serves me well for trusting a Greek and taking his word that all was fine with the car.* I left the car on the highway and went for oil at the nearest gas station.

The car burned almost as much oil as gasoline. I took the engine apart in Alice's yard and overhauled it with new pistons, rings, etc., using my engineering skills. With the better running car, I took Alice and the two boys all around Florida, including Disney World, which had just opened in Orlando.

The Ford Mercury Meteor

The long vacation over, I started to look for work. I was hired by Applied Marine Technology in Miami. The company sent me to Tampa to open a new branch there. Every Friday, I drove back to Miami to stay with Alice. On Monday, I drove back to Tampa, a trip of about five hours.

I stayed in Tampa for six months. Then the company brought me back to Miami for a major job on a ship docked there. The company needed extra engineers for the project, and I recommended a friend, Dimitrios Kareglis, a fellow Greek engineer whom I had met in the Bahamas. We started to work together on the new project, but soon found the working conditions under the supervision of the company's owner difficult.

On February 6, 1971, Dimitrios Kareglis had married Margaret, a Floridian from Bonita Springs, aboard the cruise ship the *S/S Bahama Star*, where he was serving as staff engineer.

Alice, Margaret, and Dimitrios Kareglis

After his wedding, he disembarked in Miami and, like me, applied for US citizenship.

The cruise industry in the early 1970s was still in its infancy. There were only three or four small cruise ships operating out of Miami, and there was a demand for engineering firms to fill the needs of the new industry.

The cruise ship *The Flavia*

Dimitrios's cruise ship the *S/S Bahama Star*

My cruise ship *The Freeport*

The *S/S Ariadne*

(Today, in 2010, the new cruise ships are mammoths with passenger capacities in the thousands)

I tended my resignation to Applied Marine Technology and found a temporary job with a company repairing engines.

My new employer, Motor Service, Inc., was owned by a German named Mr. Haas. Charlie, the supervisor, was a very nice Jewish man who, seeing my qualifications, was happy to have me in the firm.

It was now 1971, and although I was working in a job below my qualifications and diplomas, I was happy to be with my new family (I was not yet married) and my "Princepessa," as I called Alice.

At this time, my mother Georgia came to Miami to meet her son's lady friend (Alice) and her two small sons.

My mother liked Alice for her pleasant personality and manners, but she was not very happy with the idea of her younger son marrying a divorced woman with two children.

Nevertheless, she knew that I would do whatever I had decided regardless of her opinion or the opinions of my sisters, who were adamantly against it.

My mother stayed in Miami for a week and then flew to Hawaii to see her two daughters and grandchildren.

Alice with my mother Georgia

Alice and I got married on February 4, 1972, in a civil ceremony at the court of Miami.

Our marriage certificate

I had been in touch with both Dimitrios Kareglis, who by then had also resigned from Applied Marine Technology, and Captain Panos Giannakos, who had brought his wife Maria from Greece and was living in Freeport, Bahamas.

In June or July 1972, Dimitrios and I decided to form our own company.

Me (1972)   My partner Dimitrios Kareglis (1972)

We hired an attorney to draft the papers for our new venture as:

Professional Marine Engineering, Inc.

I became the president, Dimitrios Kareglis the vice president, and Margaret J. Kareglis the secretary. (Margaret died in 1980, and Alice took her position.)

Our new company was incorporated in August 1972, and we used Alice's home as our base and office.

(I had provided the down payment for the $35,000 purchase of the duplex Alice had been renting.)

Alice's duplex at 240-242 N.E. 114th Street, Miami, Florida

The company issued fifty shares, which were divided equally among the two partners.

We printed new business cards, brochures, and invoices. Despite our limited knowledge of English, we went to the offices of our former port engineers of the cruise lines to introduce our new company with confidence.

First we visited the port engineer of the Bahamas Cruise Lines (the former employer of Dimitrios) and introduced our new company. The port engineer was happy to see us, but he said the company was not in need of any mechanical or engineering services. Without expecting a response, he told me and Dimitrios that the only job that needed to be done was to manufacture folding beds for the new cruise ship the company had just brought to Miami. The Bahamas Cruise Lines had acquired the cruise ship the *S/S Australis* from her previous Greek owners and had renamed her *S/S Emerald Seas*. Immediately, I told him that our company was able to manufacture and install the beds. The port engineer, not expecting our proposal, agreed to give us a chance and gave our company the order to manufacture and install fifty beds on the *S/S Emerald Seas*. The new arrival was now the largest cruise ship operating from the port of Miami.

My partner and I left the office of the Bahamas Cruise Lines with our first business order of fifty Pullman beds, but we had to figure out how to manufacture them. We had a company on paper but no facilities, no tools, and no warehouse or shop.

Nevertheless, we took our wives out to celebrate our first order.

The following few days were busy as we planned our strategy. We rented an office close to the port of Miami, bought a used Ford truck (a 1962 F350), and sets of hand tools.

I designed the company's logo and incorporated the design in our new invoices.

The problem now was the manufacturing of the beds. Dimitrios told me that his former ship, the *S/S Bahama Star*, had Pullman beds in her passenger cabins. When she came in port, Dimitrios and I went aboard. After seeing the captain and other officers that we knew, I took several photos of the beds with Dimitrios's Polaroid camera and their measurements.

I made drawings for the beds and their mechanisms to be installed on the walls of the cabins on the *S/S Emerald Seas*. The first fifty beds were made out of marine plywood covered with Formica. We subcontracted the building of the beds to a Greek cabinetmaker, John Pentarakis (one of the best Greeks we had met in Miami, and with whom we became close friends). The mechanisms were also subcontracted with a machine shop, and they were chrome-plated.

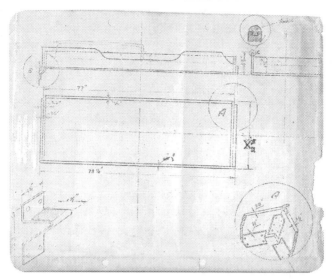

My drawing of the Pullman beds

We hired our first employees, and the installation of the beds was done while the *S/S Emerald Seas* was cruising. Bahamas Cruise Lines was happy with the work and later ordered more beds. The second order of beds was made out of aluminum frames instead of wood and Formica.

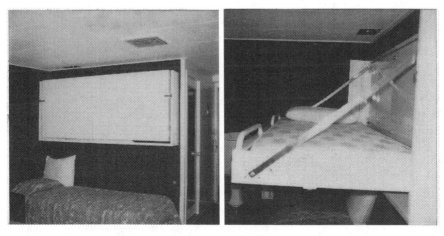

The second set of Pullman beds of aluminum construction

Thus, our new company started on good footing and in the following years prospered beyond our expectations.

During the years of operating our company, we encountered a plethora of demanding tasks and challenges, such as servicing diesel engines, steam turbines, boilers, and auxiliary machinery. We undertook great responsibilities in major ship conversions where we had to install new propulsion engines, bow thrusters, convert cargo space into passenger cabins, replace piping, steel plates, etc. They were projects for which we were not exactly trained by our schooling or by our maritime experiences on the various merchant marine vessels on which we had worked.

On February 25, 1977, we saw an announcement in the *Miami Herald* for a marshal's auction.

SECTION **B** F ★

The Miami Herald

Friday, February 25, 1977

TODAY . . .

— BOB EAST/Miami Herald Staff

WANNA BUY A BOAT? For sale to the highest bidder, one 110-foot freighter formerly used by drug smugglers who never loaded it with more than 54 tons of marijuana. Night Train is her name, and she's going on the block at noon today at U.S. Customs headquarters, 77 SE Fifth St. Minimum bid is $50,000. Marijuana bales are not included.

Dimitrios and I decided to try our luck. We went to US Customs headquarters, and I was the final bidder.

For $92,000, Dimitrios and I became shipowners. When the auction was over, the local media approached me for an interview.

Night Train to Start New Career

By FRANK GREVE
Herald Staff Writer

Two ambitious Greeks got their start as shipowners Friday, with a tramp freighter no longer useful to its late and very colorful dope-smuggling owner.

Christos Tzanetakos, 39, raised the only finger when U.S. Customs auctioneer Tony Hopkins asked $92,000 for the 110-foot Night Train. Customs and Drug Enforcement agents had seized it Feb. 1, carrying 54 tons of marijuana.

Bidding, which started at $50,000, went briskly at first in $1,000 increments. Then the standing-room, bargain-eager crowd at Customs headquarters lost interest.

TZANETAKOS took his prize modestly for himself and partner Dimitrios Kareglis. "We'll fix her and resell her or try to operate. It's our first venture and we have high hopes."

The Night Train may have been the last venture for self-styled "sailor of fortune" Harold Derber. He died of eight high-caliber pistol bullets last March in an assassination yet unsolved.

Derber gained fame in 1963 with a scheme to ferry 1,000 Cuban refugees to the U.S. at $25 to $50 a head. He gained infamy and deportation when the plot fell through and Derber lacked the refund money. Between 1965 and 1974 he remained outside the U.S. He gained readmission to Miami in 1974 as "a non-immigrant with business purposes."

Drug agency sources and Metro homicide detective James Carpenter agree Derber was a big-time smuggler who brought in marijuana by the ton. He was due to appear before the Securities and Exchange Commission in New York the day after he was murdered, to testify in a probe of stock manipulations and money laundering.

THE JUSTICE Department's Organized Crime Strike Force in Brooklyn links Derber through associates, to the late Carlo Gambino's Mafia family in New York.

According to the Canadian Registry of Shipping in St. John's, Newfoundland, Derber bought the Night Train on Nov. 11, 1974, and was its last known owner. His estate has a claim against the Customs' auction proceeds. Drug agency officials say the first of 11 dope reports involving the Night Train came in May 1975.

With former Hallandale Mayor John D. Steele, Derber and a third man were arrested Sept. 18, 1974, attempting to transfer 1.5 tons of marijuana from a warehouse near the Dade-Monroe line into a waiting truck. The charges died when Steele's lawyer, Philip Carlton Jr., showed the seizure was made without a search warrant.

"I DID not examine the past of the ship," said Tzanetakos. "We clearly had nothing to do with the previous owners or their business."

Will he change the ship's name?

"Definitely," said Tzanetakos, who didn't plan to go out Friday night to celebrate. "I'll have dinner at home," he said. "That's always the best place."

New shipowners, we were now busy bringing the ship back to working condition. We tested the Caterpillar engine and all the other machinery in the engine room and on deck (a big crane), and painted her white. Finally, we took her to a Miami drydock where her hull was cleaned and painted with antifouling paint.

The new shipowners on drydock The former *Night Train*
ready to start a new career

With all the repairs and tests completed, we listed her for sale.

Our investment and labor was rewarded when an Alaskan fisherman, Mr. Irving Tormala of Bristol Bay, Alaska, bought her for $310,000.

Mr. Tormala was in the salmon fishing business, and he used the former *Night Train* as mother ship. He renamed her *Crusader*.

Fishing flotilla aids local economy

Professional Marine Engineering became known in maritime circles, and our customers expanded to include most of the cruise lines of the time, as well as the government of the Bahamas. The Nassau Port Authority operated several tugboats and a small cargo vessel, or a tender, to supply acetylene cylinders for the navigation lights in the Bahamas.

Our company had the exclusive contract to service and refill the cylinders until the Bahamian government upgraded the navigation lights to solar and battery-operated systems. We also provided parts and engineering services for the tugboats and the Nassau harbor facilities.

The story of how Dimitrios and I bought our first new Cadillac automobiles is amusing. The port of Nassau was getting more and bigger cruise ships, and they needed fenders for the docks. They asked us if our company could provide them with large used truck tires to be used for fenders. As with the first job of the Pullman beds, we asked how many tires the Port Authority needed. We received a first order for 500 used tires.

Dimitrios and I visited the service facilities of the largest concrete-mixed cement company, and the shop supervisors were happy to let our crew take all the used tires from their yards at no cost. Well, the port of Nassau got their fender tires for $50 per tire, and Dimitrios and I got our new Cadillacs. The year was 1974.

In September1975, we formed a second corporation under the name:

Technical Marine Associates, Inc.

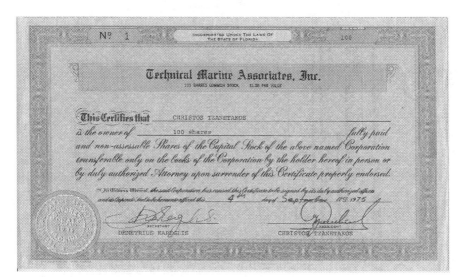

With the new corporation we planned to expand our activities into the ship brokerage and consulting business.

I invited Mr. Paul Grant to become part of the new corporation. I had served with him on the *M/V Freeport*, and we had become good friends.

We made new brochures incorporating the two corporations.

Technical Marine Associates, Inc. lasted only a few years. In the brokerage sector, we sold a small landing craft vessel to the Bahamian government whose future maintenance was carried out by our Professional Marine Engineering Service company.

With the dissolution of Technical Marine Associates, Mr. Paul Grant left the company. Dimitrios and I bought back Paul's shares in Technical Marine Associates. We remained very good friends, and when Mr. Grant became an executive of Royal Caribbean Cruise Lines, he provided many profitable jobs to Professional Marine Engineering.

We operated our business from various locations in Miami until the purchase of our own property at 272 N.E. 60th Street in Miami. The property was on two lots. On one lot was a small house with two bedrooms, a living room, a bathroom, and a kitchen. It was constructed in 1924 with wooden floors, which were still in perfect condition. The location, in an industrial area of Miami, was ideal for our business. It was only a few miles from the port.

We painted the house and converted the bedrooms into offices and the living room into a reception area with a desk for our secretary.

On the other lot, we built a 4,000 square foot building divided into two separate warehouses with a small office and bathroom for each. We used one of the warehouses for our machinery and workshop, and the other one was rented for extra income.

My partner Dimitrios (left) in front of our warehouses

In January 1981, I traveled alone to Greece to inspect a small cargo vessel that was laid off at anchor in the port of Chalkis, the capital city of Evia Island, north of Athens. Chalkis was the hometown of Dimitrios.

Dimitrios and I had decided to venture again into the business of ship ownership. We were friends with an Italian, Lillio Onorati, who operated a small maritime shipping business from Miami with good connections in the Caribbean islands.

I sent Dimitrios and Onorati a good report on the 1,500 ton cargo vessel, and the three of us became partners on the new vessel, which we bought for $120,000 (a fantastic price for a vessel in her condition). I stayed in Greece for about a month (my longest time away from Alice and the family) to close the deal, do the necessary repairs, and find a crew for our small cargo vessel. We renamed her *Venere*, a name chosen by Lillio Onorati, which in Italian means Aphrodite or Venus.

The *M/V Venere*

Lillio Onorati chartered the vessel to a company in the Dominican Republic for two years with the option to purchase the vessel at the end of the charter.

The *Venere* was a very successful enterprise for us. We not only had a good share of the charter for two years, but at the end of the charter the *Venere* was sold to the charterers for a very profitable price.

For me, the *Venere* was even a better deal because I paid my share with money I had in Greece. Greek laws at the time did not allow capital to leave Greece. I had sold a property I owned on the island of Aigina only a few miles from the port of Piraeus. I purchased the property while I was still seafaring and had built a home with a terrace overlooking the gulf of Saronikos. On a clear day, you could even see the Acropolis. When I decided to stay in the United States, I sold this property but left the money in a Greek bank. The *Venere* gave me the chance to get part of my capital out of Greece.

The island of Aigina in Greece   On the terrace of my Aigina house

In 1991, Alice and I bought the condo at Tiara Condominium Association on North Hutchinson Island in Ft. Pierce, about 120 miles north of Miami.

We still had the big house in Miami, which was too big for us now with the boys on their own and daughter Georgia at the University of Florida in Gainesville.

Alice in front of our house at 405 N.E. 114th Street, Miami, Florida

For the first year, we went to our condo on weekends and holidays while the Miami house was up for sale.

In 1992, we sold the house in Miami and moved permanently to Ft. Pierce. For the next three years I commuted to Miami, where I and Alice had a room in Dimitrios's house.

In 1995, Dimitrios and I decided to close the business and permanently retire. Professional Marine Engineering had been profitable business for us and had provided employment to many people in Miami. Most of all, in all the years of operation (since 1972), the company had a clear record with absolutely no accidents, in spite of the dangerous jobs we had undertaken.

I was fifty-seven years old, and Dimitrios was sixty.

Chapter 5

Christos the Philosopher and Social Reformer

Since I was young, I've been an avid reader. In my early teens I took the most pleasure in reading the adventures of the protagonists that excited my imagination and stimulated my love of travel and exploration. In my late teens though, when my mind had developed better critical thinking, I started to scrutinize the authors and their characters. In this stage of my life, I became interested in the writings of the philosophers of my native country of Greece, as well as the world philosophers.

I found the ancient Greek philosophers remarkable for their times, but I thought their ideas and concepts were incompatible with today's scientific knowledge. They nevertheless established a system of critical thinking that was the precursor for modern scientific method.

Among the giants of Greek thought, I read the works of Thalis, Anaximander, Pythagoras, Parmenides, Heraclitus, Empedocles, Anaxagoras, Protagoras, my favorite Epicurus, Leucippus, and Democritus, and finally Socrates, Plato, and Aristotle.

At first I was fascinated with the ideas of Socrates as they were written by his pupil Plato. Socrates and other Greek philosophers and writers were taught in high schools where I attended classes in Greece.

I noticed that in the dialogue of *Phaedo*, Socrates, using what we now call the Cyclical Argument, persuaded his students to accept that the soul is immortal.

To the ancient Greeks as well as religious adherents of today, soul is a separate entity from the human body that survives after death. Naturally, the ancients didn't know about computers. Similar to our brains, computers can lose the data (soul) on their hard drives after they break down or die.

To me, this human delusion of the soul and the other fantasy of God were, and still are, the most pernicious concepts of the fallible mind (brain) of man. I was convinced that we are responsible directly or indirectly for most of the calamities and atrocities that we as species have inflicted on each other and on our planet's many other species, from antiquity to present.

It was at this stage of my life that I questioned the validity of the Greek Orthodox religion of my parents. The Greek Orthodox religion was also the official religion of Greece. I studied the Bible, (Old and New Testaments) and found inconsistencies, unscientific statements, and a plethora of absurdities.

The argument that this book was inspired by an omniscient, omnipotent entity, a god, and yet contained many false statements added another reason for me to retire the Christian god as well as the gods of any other religions to the company of the Olympian gods, goddesses, and semi-gods of the past.

Since I rejected all the gods, I declared myself an atheist. Now I was a lone atheist in a country saturated with religion. *Were any other atheists in Greece?* I wondered.

To be an atheist in Greece was very dangerous, since there were laws that punished the unbelievers. I was certain that many others had come to the same conclusions, but they were keeping their atheism to themselves.

Nevertheless, the honor of arriving to the philosophy of atheism belongs to the ancient Greeks. In his book *The Life of Greece,* Will Durant credits Theodorus of Cyrene, a contemporary of Epicurus among the first atheists. He became known as the Atheist of Cyrene. Another ancient Greek atheist was Diagoras, known as the Atheist of Melos.

To my children and grandchildren, I gave the names of great atheist authors that I have read and enjoyed. I hope one day they too will read their work and study them. "If you adopt the philosophy of atheism," I advised them, "you would be in good company."

In Greece, the author Nikos Kazantzakis and poet Kostantinos P. Kavafis are world-known intellectuals and of course both atheists. Other European authors I read and admire are Emile Zola, Jean Paul Sartre, Paul Heinrich Dietrich, baron d'Holbach, Denis Diderot, Albert Camus, Anatole France, Victor Hugo, the Marquis de Sade, August Comte, and of course the philosopher Voltaire, all of whom were atheists or nonreligious adherents. I especially liked Emile Zola's statement:

> Civilization will thrive when the last stone from the last church falls on the last priest.

A similar quote comes from Denis Diderot, (chief editor of *Encyclopedie*)

> Mankind will not be free until the last king is strangled with the entrails of the last priest.

I also read and recommend Bertrand Russell, John Stuart Mill, David Hume, Henry Fielding, E. M. Forster, Samuel Butler, Carroll Lewis, Charles Darwin, George Eliot, H. G. Wells, George Orwell, D. H. Lawrence, Aldous Huxley, George Bernard Shaw, Richard Dawkins, W. Somerset Maugham, Lord Byron, Geoffrey Chaucer, Rudyard Kipling, Percy Shelley, Virginia Woolf, Joseph McCabe, Robert Louis Stevenson, Oscar Wilde, Henrik Ibsen, and Friedrich Nietzsche.

American authors I recommend are Mark Twain (who said, "*I had read the Bible completely by the age of fifteen and its impurity had soiled my mind*"), John Steinbeck, Pearl S. Buck, Jack London, Richard P. Feynman, B. F. Skinner, H. L. Mencken, Ayn Rand, Arthur Miller, Gore Vidal, Kurt Vonnegut, Pete Hamill, T. S. Eliot, Ambrose Bierce, and Ernest Hemingway (who said: *All thinking men are atheists*).

On birthdays, I gave my daughter Georgia books as presents.

With my daughter Georgia on her twentieth birthday

One of the greatest books I have given to my daughter is *Man and His Gods* by Homer W. Smith with a foreword by Albert Einstein. I think this book is the most comprehensive history of the religious ideas of humankind.

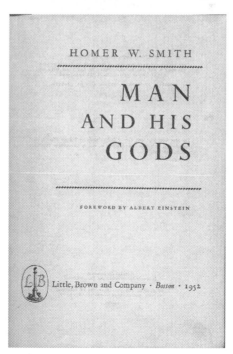

My favorite philosophers are Bertrand Russell and Friedrich Nietzsche.

The more intense has been the religion of any period and the more profound has been the dogmatic belief, the greater has been the cruelty and the worst has been the state of affairs.— Bertrand Russell

*A thorough reading and understanding the Bible is the surest path to atheism.—*Friedrich Nietzsche

Reading the biographies of great writers and scientists also gave me many hours of pleasure. Among them, I cherish Albert Einstein's biography *Einstein: His Life and Universe* by Walter Isaacson (given to me by my daughter on a Father's Day), *Genius,* the biography of Richard P. Feynman (my favorite scientist and philosopher) by James Gleik, the biographical novel of Charles Darwin entitled *The Origin* by Irving Stone, and several biographies of my beloved Mark Twain.

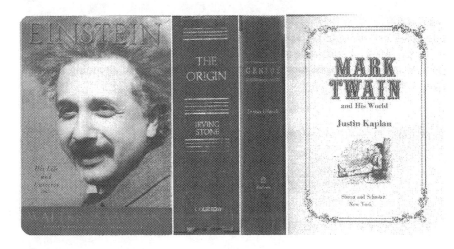

Biographies of great men and women are not only very interesting reading material, but studying them is an excellent source of learning and understanding the history of our species.

In the 1970s, Alice and I took the family to Greek affairs held in halls of Greek churches, such as annual festivals or Christmas and Easter dances. The food was good, and the Greek folk dancing and music reminded me of my native Greece. Nevertheless, Alice and I were lonely atheists.

I found the United States and its people to be very religious. Alice and I felt like aliens from another planet.

Then in the late 1970s while I was driving and listening to the radio, I happened to switch on a radio show whose host had on Madalyn Murray O'Hair, an atheist, as his guest. Madalyn, I learned, was the founder of the first atheist organization in the United States.

I was thrilled listening to this dynamic woman who was not afraid to proclaim her atheism to the world. What I heard that day set the course of my atheist activities. During the talk show, Madalyn O'Hair gave the phone number of her organization, American Atheists, whose headquarters was in Austin, Texas. I scribbled the number down on a paper pad. Soon after my return home from my office, I called the Texas number and got more information on the organization. To my pleasant surprise, I learned that American Atheists had a chapter serving the Miami and Ft. Lauderdale areas. Alice and I became members of the chapter and started attending the monthly meetings.

Me with Madalyn O'Hair

In 1982, I was elected chapter director, a position I held until the closing of the chapter in July 1991.

Like all the other members of American Atheists in the United States (about 2,500 members at the time), Alice and I admired Madalyn for bringing atheism into the open. In 1963, she won a landmark lawsuit that reached the Supreme Court of the United States. The court voted 8-1 in Madalyn Murray's favor, banning prayer and Bible recitation in public schools in the United States.

My admiration and support for Madalyn lasted until 1986, when she arbitrarily and against the official articles of the organization and the laws of the United States for nonprofit organizations, established her son Jon Garth Murray as president for life. I had earlier accepted an invitation to be on the board in one of the five corporations under the umbrella of American Atheists. Now I realized that even my position as vice president of the United Secularists of America, Inc., was illegal, since I was appointed to this position by Madalyn. I obtained the IRS booklet, publication 557, *Tax-Exempt Status for Your Organization,* and thoroughly studied its content.

I realized that all nonprofit membership organizations are required by law to elect their board of directors by their members at the annual meetings, or again from the members by mail ballots. The law also specifies that board members of 501(c)(3) nonprofit organizations cannot draw salaries. Board members and officers can only be reimbursed for any expenses they encounter during their terms and duties. Now familiar with the laws and regulations of nonprofit 501(c)(3) tax exempt organization such as the American Atheists, I took a closer look at their operation. I found out that the Murray family (Madalyn, her son Jon Garth, and granddaughter Robin) were the three directors in all of the corporations under the umbrella of American Atheists. The other two directors on each corporation were rubber stamp directors appointed by the family. I realized that the Murray family had absolute control. American Atheists was a totalitarian and nepotistic organization.

Another violation of the articles of the organization and the IRS rules was that Jon Murray and Robin Murray were paid employees of American Atheists. Madalyn mentioned their salaries several times when she solicited funds; however, in their 990 forms she reported their compensation as zero. Of course, if someone is a paid employee of a 501(c)(3) organization, such as an executive director, he or she cannot be on the board of directors as well.

Finally, I found that there was no accountability of the finances of the organization. In spite of all of the violations, I naively thought that I could persuade the Murrays to comply with the laws and bring democratization to the American Atheists. I sent letters to Madalyn and Jon encouraging them to have elections for the board of directors and comply with the IRS rules. My constructive criticism was met with vitriolic answers.

Disappointed and disgusted with the ignorance, arrogance, and stupidity of Madalyn and Jon Murray, I resigned from the board of the United Secularists of America, Inc., but not from my position as chapter director of the South Florida Chapter of American Atheists, where I had been duly elected by its members. My plan was to challenge the O'Hairs at the next annual convention of American Atheists, inform the members of the violations, and demand compliance.

Meanwhile, other chapter directors around the United States had similar objections and demands for the O'HairsMurrays. Even with all of the opposition, Madalyn O' Hair, her son Jon, and granddaughter Robin thought that they could continue their illegal operation by closing the local chapters of American Atheists. In 1991, without notifying me and the board of the South Florida chapter, Jon Murray sent a letter to the bank where the chapter had its account, closed the account, and took the balance of $6,200.

After the O'Hairs had the money, Jon Murray sent a letter to the chapter informing the members of their decision to close all of the chapters of American Atheists. When I was informed by the treasurer of the chapter that the chapter's account was stolen by the O'Hairs, I was infuriated.

I called for a meeting of all of the Florida members of the chapter (about eighty at the time), and we decided to form our own atheist organization. I drafted the articles of incorporation and bylaws and sent them to the members of approval and suggestions. I designed the new organization's logo and filed for its incorporation. On January 28, 1992, Atheists of Florida, Inc. was incorporated in the state of Florida and received its status as a nonprofit tax exempt organization.

E Pluribus Unum became the official motto of the organization.

As founder and elected president of Atheists of Florida, I immediately drafted a complaint with the IRS enumerating all of the violations of the O'Hair family and requesting their investigation into the matter.

ATHEISTS OF FLORIDA, INC.

P.O. BOX 530102
MIAMI, FL 33153-0102

Phone: (305) 936-0210

DEPARTMENT OF THE TREASURY
INTERNAL REVENUE SERVICE
CRIMINAL INVESTIGATION DIVISION
ATRIUM WEST, SUITE 231
7771 W. OAKLAND PK. BLVD.
SUNRISE, FLORIDA 33351
Attn: Mr. MICHAEL P. SCHEFFER
Special Agent   March 8th, 1993

Dear Mr. Scheffer,

Pursuant to my visit at your office, March 6th, 1993, and our subsequent conversation pertaining to the complaint of our organization as enumerated in the submitted exhibits, ATHEISTS OF FLORIDA, INC. respectfully petitions your intervention in bringing all the Not For Profit organizations under the umbrella of American Atheists of Austin Texas in compliance with the law.

Respectfully,

Christos Tzanetakos
President.

File:Complaint
Disk: aof 98.2
February 10, 1993

COMPLAINT

Pursuant to FS 617.2003. , ATHEISTS OF FLORIDA, INC. a Nonprofit Florida Organization, organized under the FS Not For Profit Corporation Act 617,alleges as follows:

1. That Madalyn O Hair, Jon G. Murray and Robin Murray O Hair, (The family) have violated the members' rights by inuring the power of S.O.S. Inc (Society of Separation, Inc) a tax exempt membership organization . They also inured the power of all the tax exempt organizations under the umbrella of American Atheists, by establishing themselves arbitrarily as the three out of the five directors of the above Not For Profit organizations, contrary to article 5 of the original articles of S.O.S. Inc and the Florida Not For Profit Corporation Act.

FS 617.0834

A transaction from which the officers or directors derived an improper personal benefit, either directly or indirectly.

FS 617.0803 Number of Directors:

Directors shall be elected or appointed in the manner and in the terms provided in the articles of incorporation or the bylaws. (provided the bylaws are in compliance to the law)

(See Article 5. of the original articles of S.O.S. Inc. Exhibit I)

The business and prudential affairs of this corporation(S.O.S. Inc) shall be managed and controlled by a board of five directors to be elected annually.

2. The family drafted bylaws (Exhibit II) inconsistent with the law FS 617.0206 Bylaws , and article 5 of the original articles of incorporation.

FS 617.0206 Bylaws

The initial bylaws of a corporation shall be adopted by its board of directors. The power to alter, amend, or repeal the bylaws or adopt new bylaws shall be vested in the board of directors unless otherwise provided in the articles of incorporation or the bylaws.
The bylaws may contain any provision for the regulation and management of the affairs of the corporation NOT INCONSISTENT with the law or the articles of incorporation.

3. The family violated the rights of the South Florida Chapter when they refused to comply with the recommendations made by the Elected director of the chapter, Christos Tzanetakos, for the implementation of article 5 of the original articles, and since the Society of Separationists Inc. was authorized to contact business in the state of Florida. (see Exhibit A) to conform with FS 617.0803 Not For Profit Corporation Act. (see exhibit III. Letter to Madalyn O Hair, exhibit IV, O Hair's reply , and exhibits V, VI, VII and VIII) correspondence of chapter director's resignation from the national board.

4. The family violated the rights of the South Florida Chapter (now Atheists of Florida, Inc.) when the chapter director requested the compliance of the law and the original article 5 of the organization (S.O.S. Inc) from the arbitrarily appointed president Jon G. Murray. (He was established as president by Madalyn O' Hair)
see exhibit IX.

5. The Family violated the rights of the members of the South Florida Chapter (now Atheists of Florida, Inc.) when the ELECTED officers of the chapter in response to a request by the chapter coordinator Don Sanders of Houston (now deceased) who had demanded the inclusion of the signature of one of the family members (the Murrays) on the chapter's bank account, sent a letter signed by all the elected officers , requesting the financial accountability of the Murrays as mandated by the IRS rules for 501(c)(3) organizations. (see exhibit X letter to Don Sanders)

6. The family violated the rights of the South Florida Chapter (now Atheists of Florida, Inc.) when Jon G. Murray acting as president and without any notification to the officers of the chapter, closed the bank account of the chapter, by providing fraudulent and contradictory statements to the bank, and only when they (the family) secured the $6,260.00 balance of the South Florida chapter's account, Jon G. Murray notified the director with a letter dated July 19, 1991. (see exhibit XI corporate resolution, exhibit XII letter to Southeast bank, and exhibit XIII letter dated July 19, 91 to director Christos Tzanetakos.)

7. The family violated the rights of the South Florida Chapter (now Atheists of Florida, Inc.) by closing the P.O. Box of the chapter without notification to the elected officers, diverting the mail to Austin TX and isolating the members from their officers.

8. The family violated the rights of the members of ATHEISTS OF FLORIDA, INC. (the organization which was formed by the officers and the unanimous resolution of independence as stated on page 3 of the original articles of Atheists of Florida, Inc.) when Jon G. Murray ignored the official request of Atheists of Florida, Inc. for the return of its funds. (see exhibit XIV Articles and bylaws, exhibit XV resolution and exhibit XVI letter of 09/03/1992.)

Submitted for ATHEISTS OF FLORIDA, INC. by:

Christos Tzanetakos
President

The events that followed proved that Madalyn Murray O' Hair was after all an empress without clothes and a common criminal.

I was convinced that the IRS started their investigation and the Murrays tried to flee the country. I learned that they already had an account in New Zealand where they were planning to flee. Jon Garth Murray attempted to cash the money of the organization in gold bullions, but a criminal who was hired by the family to work at the Atheist Center in Austin, Texas named David Roland Waters murdered Madalyn Murray O' Hair, her son Jon, and granddaughter Robin. Waters placed their dismembered bodies in barrels and dumped them in a Texas field. The family was missing for long time until the mystery of their disappearance was solved by the arrest and conviction of David Roland Waters, who led the authorities to the dismembered bodies in the Texas field.

Despite my disappointment with the Murrays and American Atheists, I never lost my enthusiasm for atheism and in particular my adherence to the First Amendment of the United States Constitution. Under my leadership, Atheists of Florida became a champion for the separation of church and state.

Meanwhile, in other states, other former chapters of American Atheists had formed new atheist organizations. In 1993, the new independent atheist organizations around the country came together in a historic meeting in Los Angeles, California, to form an alliance. I flew to California with the vice president of Atheists of Florida, Inc., Ed Golly, to represent our Florida organization.

I was elected co-president of the new organization, Atheist Alliance, Inc., and served for two consecutive terms. During my two years of service, Atheists Alliance, Inc. expanded its membership of independent atheists organizations from the original five to ten. One of the prerequisites for membership to Atheists Alliance was for the applicant organizations to have a democratic constitution in compliance to the regulations for 501(c)(3) tax exempt organizations. Today (2010), Atheist Alliance is an international organization with member organizations all over the world (fourteen foreign countries and thirty-two US organizations).

For the first six years of Atheists of Florida, Inc., I served as founder and president. Then, adherent to my principles for democratic governance, I introduced an amendment to the bylaws of Atheists of Florida limiting the position of the president to a maximum of two consecutive terms.

Thus, having established Atheists of Florida, Inc., on good footing with a membership of about 300 members from Key West to Tallahassee, I passed the leadership to the next generation. Nevertheless, I remained on the board, and in 1995 I founded the Mark Twain Scholarship Fund. The fund was the official scholarship of Atheists of Florida, Inc. I introduced the name of the scholarship in honor of my beloved author Samuel Clemens, better known as Mark Twain. I designed the logo of the scholarship with the bust of Mark Twain surrounded by a laurel wreath.

The logo of the Mark Twain Scholarship Fund

Next I composed a brochure describing the scholarship and who was eligible, and the disclosure of the organization's 501(c)(3) status for potential donors to claim any donations on their tax returns.

For the introduction "Why Mark Twain?" I used my daughter's high school paper entitled "Mark Twain' s Perspective on Man and His God."

I sent The Mark Twain Scholarship Fund brochures and applications to all of the universities in the state of Florida. In the following years, I introduced the scholarship to universities nationwide using the Internet.

I chose this motto for the scholarship:

It Is Better To Light A Candle Than To Curse The Darkness

I operated the Mark Twain Scholarship as founder and trustee from its inception in 1995 until February 2006 when the corporation was dissolved.

In 1997, I applied to the Miami Public Access TV system to produce half-hour programs for the Mark Twain Scholarship. My application was accepted, and I produced twelve half-hour TV programs that were aired in Dade County and later in the Tampa area for the public access system.

Mark Twain Scholarship Forum

To promote post secondary education in the fields of arts and humanities, education, science, engineering and law, the Mark Twain Scholarship Fund is sponsoring *The Mark Twain Scholarship Forum*. The organization provides scholarship grants to qualified students who choose any of these fields.

Christos Tzanetakos, Producer

The Mark Twain Scholarship Forum's topics include "Contemporary Ideas on Evolution," "Nietzche," "Ethics and Morality," "The Power of Prayer," and "Book Banning."

The Mark Twain Scholarship Forum airs Mondays at 12:00 p.m., Tuesdays at 5:00 p.m. and Wednesdays at 10:00 p.m. on Cable-TAP Community Station 36.

I submitted the Mark Twain TV programs to the Alliance for Community Media, and I received first place in the 1997 Sweetheart Video Festival.

I also entered the TV programs into the 1997 Southeast Region of the Alliance for Community Media Sunshine Video Festival held in Tampa, Florida, and again I was awarded for Outstanding Community Programming.

In all, I produced sixty TV programs; forty—eight for Atheists of Florida, and twelve for the Mark Twain Scholarship Fund. I placed all the programs on DVDs, which are stored in my personal archives as well as in the archives of Atheists of Florida, Inc.

As founder and chairman of the Mark Twain Scholarship, I delivered the annual messages for the fund's annual reports.

Samuel Langhorne
Clemens - Mark Twain

Christos Tzanetakos, Founder
of the Mark Twain Scholarship
Program

The 2005 Message

Since the founding of the Mark Twain Scholarship in 1995, I have tried to address humankind's most urgent problems in my chairman's report. This year, with the insanity of war still raging in Iraq, with other conflicts around the globe, and recently the burning of the Danish and Norwegian embassies by fanatical Muslims whose religious fervor was ignited by the publishing of cartoons in the Danish newspaper *Jyllands-Posten*, I thought it most appropriate to incorporate my report with a photo. The photo is of the thought-provoking artwork of Mr. Norman B. Leclair, long-time member of Atheists of Florida and generous supporter of the Mark Twain Scholarship Fund.

Mr. Leclair's sculpture composition entitled *Reflections of a Dodo* consists of a round base on a pedestal covered with a photo of our

Earth as seen from space. A human skull representing humankind is placed in front of three mirrors reflecting Judaism (star of David), Christianity (cross), and the Muslim religion (crescent moon). On the base of the skull the caption reads:

"We Have Met the Enemy and He is Us"

If I could contribute something to the most provocative art work of Mr. Leclair, I would add one more mirror reflecting the fourth impostor: *nationalism.*

Reflecting now to the cartoon and judging from the burning of the Danish and Norwegian embassies and the death threats against the Danish cartoonist by Muslim extremists (naturally adherents of any faith never wondered why their omnipotent gods failed them, e.g., (Holocaust,) or allow puny humans to do their dirty work, e.g., (assassin abortion doctors, 9/11, etc. etc.

Similar to Leclair, the cartoonist Parker created a very profound cartoon.

In the cartoon a soldier is consulting a fortune teller. She looks into her crystal ball and tells him: "I see a time when peace shall reign throughout the world."

"I bet the people are happy," he happily exclaims.

"I don't see any people," the somewhat baffled fortune teller retorts.

In 2005, the scholarship received seventy-one applications and essays from all around the nation on the following topic:

E. M. Forster wrote, "I do not believe in belief." Pete Hamill called "belief the great killer. Political belief has slaughtered millions. Religious belief has slaughtered the rest." How relevant are these quotes in our present world affairs?

Eight students received grants totalling $3,200 and seventy-one applicants received a free copy of Bertrand Russell's essay "Why I Am Not a Christian." The essays of these young students were most enlightening, and I hope and wish that their generation will unmask the "four impostors" before their destructive role leads humankind to its premature extinction.

The 2004 Message

Two-time Pulitzer Prize–winning historian Barbara W. Tuchman begins her monumental work *The March of Folly* with the statement: "Mankind (Humankind), it seems, makes a poorer performance of government than most any other Human activityIn this sphere, wisdom, which may be defined as the exercise of judgment acting on experience, common sense and available information, is less operative and more frustrated than it should be. Why do holders of high office so often act contrary to the way reason points and enlightened self-interest suggest? Why does intelligent mental process seem so often not to function?"

At present, it seems the United States and indeed many parts of the world are on a march of folly, which, if not reversed soon, would lead to the degradation of our planet or even a premature extinction of our species.

An analysis of George W. Bush's inaugural address can give us clues as to why this individual and his four-year march of folly have already plunged our country into the quagmire of war with Iraq (considered by many a second Vietnam).

Opening his address, George W. Bush acknowledged the invited religious representatives as "reverend clergy." f course, these are the individuals (Christians and others) responsible for the perpetuation of irrational dogmatic ideologies that feed hatred and excuse murder (naturally they claim otherwise). To enumerate the religious wars of the past or the acts of religious fanaticism of the present in the form of murdering abortion doctors, bombing clinics, flying airplanes into civilian buildings or exploding themselves to kill others would be redundant.

George W. Bush said: "The best hope for peace in our world is the expansion of freedom in all the world." While this sounds grandiose, it is indeed correct. One wonders, however, how the author of the above can reconcile his family's close ties with the regime of Saudi Arabia, where freedom is restricted and women in particular are not allowed even to drive an automobile.

"From the day of our founding, we have proclaimed that every man and woman on this earth has rights, and dignity, and matchless value, because they bear the image of the maker of Heaven and Earth . . . because no one is fit to be a master, and no one to be a slave." Apparently, George W. Bush and his speechwriters forgot that the institution of slavery was in practice long after the founding of the country, and a universal declaration of human Rights established after World War II. They seem to have forgotten that segregation was abolished only within the last fifty years. Yet no god or goddess did anything to ameliorate the suffering of the slaves in the past or the victims of natural or man-made calamities of today.

"America will not impose our own style of government on the unwilling." Yet George W. Bush, obsessed by his religious paranoia and his calling to spread Christianity and democracy, has devastated Iraq, murdered thousands of its citizens who had absolutely nothing to do with 9/11, and created a climate of terror epitomized by his arrogant statement: "Some have unwisely chosen to test America's resolve and found it firm."

His declaration at the United Nations that "with or without their approval, America will proceed to the war" will remain infamous, and history will term it a gross violation of international law, as well as a violation to our own Constitution.

"We honor your friendship, we rely on your counsel," (apparently only if they go along with the Bush doctrine of pre-emptive wars.).

"Americans, at our best, value the life we see in one another and must remember that even the unwanted have worth."

The human rights abuses at Abu Ghraib and Guantanamo prisons unequivocally contradict this statement, cast us in a shameful light, and further enflame the hate against us.

The truth of the matter is that our government has been hijacked by the religious fundamentalist zealots who succeeded to elevate one of their kind to the highest office in our land. If we want to spread the idea and ideals of our constitutionally-governed democracy, we must strengthen the United Nations whose charter, if followed by all and in particular the United States, can bring justice and peace on our planet. By acting unilaterally as bullies, we are damaging our country and jeopardizing the stability of the rest of the world.

As long as we react to attacks against us only with force without investigating and acknowledging the underlying reasons for the hatred against us, (mainly our failed foreign policies), and as long as we allow the impostors of religion and nationalism to influence or control our politics, America and the rest of the world will remain in the darkness of terror.

In an attempt to assist and enlighten our young generation, the Mark Twain Scholarship Fund continued its program by giving out eight grants to students totaling $3,200 for their tuition needs in 2004. Also, the fund provided a free copy of Bertrand Russell's essay *Why I Am Not a Christian* to all sixty-one applicants.

The 2004 essays present a gleam of encouragement that the new generation (provided that we survive this march of folly) will produce leaders whose decisions will be based on reason, science, and the rule of international law instead of the paranoia of dogmatic religious beliefs.

The 2003 Message

Ten years ago, the late astronomy Professor Carl Sagan wrote an article entitled, "Is There Intelligent Life on Earth?" In it, he narrates the findings of imaginary aliens who, while entering our solar system, discovered our blue planet. From their orbital point they witness with utter dismay that the dominant organism was 'simultaneously destroying their ozone layer and their forest, eroding their topsoil and performing massive, uncontrolled experiments on their planet's climate.'

Dr. Sagan concluded that "perhaps it is time to reassess the hypothesis that there is intelligent life on Earth." He stopped short, however, of imagining that these visitors, curious to decipher the reasons for this peculiar behavior of the dominant organism, decided to land their spaceship and further investigate the poisoning and degradation of the planet's life.

The leader of the blue planet expedition entered the following in her log:

"Having detected from our orbiting observation that the dominant organism possess destructive weapons, nuclear and others, or weapons of mass destruction (WMD) as they call them, we decided to land on a remote and uninhabited part of the planet.

After securing and concealing our spaceship, we proceeded cautiously exploring the surrounding terrain, which was beaming with a variety of life forms other than the dominant one. We encountered many of these, some permanently attached to the ground, others roaming, and a variety of others flying in the air. At a nearby large concentration of water, we detected similar conditions with species attached to the bottom of the underwater terrain, others crawling around and a large number swimming through the various depths.

Convinced that neither of these species was in any way connected with the destruction we witnessed from orbit, the expedition proceeded towards a place where a large concentration of the dominant organism was previously detected.

Taking all precautions not to be recognized, we were soon able to mingle with them and gradually, listening and watching their activities, we came to understand their languages.

It was from this point, that our expedition became more fascinating. Our search took us through the various land masses or 'Continents' as they name them, where the 'humans' as the dominant organism call themselves, have established individual territories called 'countries.'

They are remarkable creatures; in their relatively short appearance on their planet, they are the only ones who developed a substantial civilization with advances in the arts and sciences, which makes the puzzle of self-destruction even more profound.

Our search brought us to places where the humans are occupied killing each other, destroying their cities and their surrounding countryside. The paradox of killings was more puzzling in a place called "Palestine" by one group and 'Israel' by another where both warring groups claim ancestry from the same person named Abraham.

In a nearby country called 'Iraq' we discovered the traces of a recent war (1991 according to their calendar) in which some of the most technologically advanced countries, after supplying, or more correctly exchanging their destructive weapons with this country's oil wealth, jointly attacked them; they buried alive thousands of its citizens in their desert trenches, and caused massive fires from the oil wells, some of which were ignited by their bombs and others which were deliberately set on fire by the attacked Iraqis.

The neighboring country called 'Iran' is similarly scarred by a war waged not long ago by these two groups of Humans, in which, besides the innumerable deaths, thousands were maimed for life by the use of chemical weapons.

We continued our investigation to the rest of the planet, and found many more places where the humans are engaged in this insane practice of war. We also studied the past, which shows that this disease has been with them throughout their written history.

With our investigation completed, we finalized our conclusion for this planet's degradation to the following three man made ideas or concepts.

NATIONALISM

This concept which divides the humans in groups of common allegiance and most often in hostility against each other, is based on the different forms of government, local cultures, and what they call 'races'. This last division is justified on grounds of facial characteristics or skin color, although, DNA examinations from all these allegedly different 'races' revealed a common source.

RELIGION

We spent a substantial amount of time studying this extraordinary and strictly human phenomenon. Broadly speaking, religion is a set of unsubstantiated theories or 'beliefs' as the humans call them, going beyond or contrary to the evidence.

We encountered numerous major religions and innumerable smaller ones. (incidentally, all claiming to be the one and only true religion).

A common concept of all religions is the acceptance of an entity beyond the physical universe called 'God' who created the whole universe out of *nothing*. At first this naive and simplistic idea seems quite harmless, but many notions attached to this main concept are the roots of the most divisive and destructive force on this planet.

The adherents of each religion are fanatically attached to their dogmas and they will use coercive methods, mental or physical, to impose their beliefs on others.

We found that many of the wars of the past and similarly the current conflicts on this planet are caused by religious differences.

The acceptance among all religions that man is a special creation of their gods, (allegedly he made them in his image), encouraged the domination of all the other living matter by man, leading to the present catastrophic explosion of their numbers, and the decline or extinction of many of the other species.

On a personal note, I would like to emphasize my feelings pertaining to the effects of this insidious practice upon the female gender of this species. I was shocked to find out that almost all religions debased females, relegating them to non-person status.

GREED

This strictly individual human vice, is independent from the previous two, Nationalism and Religion. Individuals or groups of them infected by this disease, (most humans are), although they know that their lives are finite, strive to accumulate as much wealth as possible; so strong is this compulsion, that in its pursuit, individually or in groups, they will exploit their fellow humans, subjecting them to the most cruel and degrading conditions. They will even influence governments to initiate wars, if this will bring them more wealth.

It is greed that leads them to the massive destruction of their planet as we observed from orbit and on site, by cutting their forests, scarring their land with monstrous mining machines, polluting their rivers, lakes, oceans and atmosphere with their factories and the ever increasing human waste due to the continuous overpopulation promoted and encouraged by their religious beliefs as we have already previously explained.

IS THERE HOPE FOR THEIR FUTURE?

We calculated that the blue planet will be in existence for another 4-5 billion years, until the central star of this planetary system loses its life-giving energy.

In our brief visit here we found that a small segment of the human population came to realize that "Man is personally responsible for what he is and what he does; that there are no values external to man and no given human nature which he is obliged to fulfill; that man chooses his values and makes himself, and may therefore choose to be a different person."

Whether they succeed in influencing and enlightening their fellow man, . . . to be seen.

End of the report

The 2002 Message

2002 was yet another year for reflection on the causes and horrors of wars. In the wake of the 9/11 disaster, the leadership of our own government is threatening humankind with another conflict, setting the stage for a new era of terror and the death of our civil and human rights as we knew them before the World Trade Center and the Pentagon attacks. Now the war drums are again reverberating from Washington and, as often is the case, religion and nationalism are used to fuel the flames.

Shall we ever learn from the horrible business of war?

Since the dawn of history, many thinkers have condemned war as a business in which men and now women are sent to die in or die to enrich others. To my knowledge, no other thinker portrayed the atrocities and the horrors of war more profoundly than the Greek poet Euripides in his tragic play *The Trojan Women*. Euripides, an Athenian citizen and patriot, condemns war and the victorious Greeks who, after the fall of Troy, went on a rampage of senseless killings of Trojans, burned Troy, and enslaved their women and children. To Euripides, no other suffering approaches that which war inflicts.

It seems humankind never learned that inevitably both victors and vanquished suffer together in the end. Then, as now, warmongers practice the policy that soldiers must not think. Anyone who reasons and asks why is treasonous in the military. Above all, they must not think about the rights and wrongs of the war. Athens called that being unpatriotic, not to mention traitorous. Is our present government treating war dissenters any better today? Perhaps our government and the majority of our fellow Americans who favor a new war with Iraq or any other adversary should be reminded of Athens and its conflict with a Greek island. According to the historian Thucydides, an island ally of Athens revolted during the Peloponnesian war. "Athens sent a big fleet against her and captured her, and in furious anger voted to put all the men to death and make slaves of the women and children. They dispatched a ship to carry the order to the general in command, and then, true to the spirit of the city that was still so great, they realized the shocking thing they had done, and they sent another boat to try to overtake the first and bring it back, or, if that was impossible, to get to the island in time to prevent the massacre. We are told how the rowers rowed as none ever before, and how they did arrive in time. And Athens felt that weight of guilt lifted, and rejoiced."

Today, we don't need to row hard to send a message. Can our government and the American people regain the glory of what the United States stands for and send a message of peace instead of threats of war? In closing, can our country regain the respect of the world and rise again to the ideals of its founders?

The 2001 Message

With the dawn of the twenty-first century and the new millennium, the prospects for a more rational era were quite promising. Pacifists around the globe (myself included) were celebrating the efforts of solving world conflicts by diplomatic negotiations and through the interpretation of international law under the aegis of the United Nations. Then, on September 11, our nation and the world received a terrible wake-up call.

The Dream was just a Dream

Now, our Department of Justice in the hands of a born-again Christian fanatic

Attorney General John Ashcroft

and our Department of Defense (since World War II it has been used mostly for offense) headed by another Christian Taliban (Donald Rumsfeld),

War criminals Rumsfeld and Bush

Mark Twain's "War Prayer" resonates in our minds:

"It was a time of great exulting and excitement. The country was up in arms, the war was on, in every breast burned the holy fire of patriotism; the drums were beating, the bands playing, the toy pistols popping, the bunched firecrackers hissing and sputtering; on every hand and far down the receding and fading spread of roofs and balconies a fluttering wilderness of flags flashed in the sun; daily the young volunteers marched down the wide avenue gay and fine in their new uniforms, the proud fathers and mothers and sisters and sweethearts cheering them with voices choked with happy emotion as they swung by; nightly the packed mass meetings listened, panting, to patriot oratory which stirred the deepest depths of their hearts, and which they interrupted at briefest intervals with cyclones of applause, the tears running down their cheeks the while; in the churches the pastors preached devotion to flag and country, and invoked the God of Battles, beseeching His aid in our good cause in outpourings of fervid eloquence which moved every listener. It was indeed a glad and gracious time, and the half dozen rash spirits that ventured to disapprove of the war and cast doubt upon its righteousness straight way got such a stern and angry warning that for their personal safety's sake they quickly shrank out of sight and offended no more in that way.

On to the war

O Lord our Father, our young patriots, idols of our hearts, go forth to battle—be Thou near them! With them—in spirit—we also go forth from the sweet peace of our beloved firesides to smite the foe.

O Lord our God, help us to tear their soldiers to bloody shreds with our shells; help us to cover their smiling fields with the pale forms of their patriot dead; help us to drown the thunder of the guns with shrieks of their wounded, writhing in pain; help us to lay waste their humble homes with hurricanes of fire.

Help us to wring the hearts of their unoffending widows with unavailing grief; help us to turn them out roofless with their little children to wander unfriended the wastes of their desolated land in rags and hunger and thirst, sports of the sun flames of summer and the icy winds of winter, broken in spirit, worn with travail, imploring Thee for the refuge of the grave and denied it—for our sakes who adore Thee, Lord, blast their hopes, blight their lives, protract their bitter pilgrimage, make heavy their steps, water their way with tears, stain the white snow with the blood of their wounded feet! We ask it, in the spirit of love, of Him Who is the Source of Love, and who is the ever-faithful refuge and friend of all that are sore beset and seek his aid with humble and contrite hearts. Amen."

In closing, can our country and the world escape the tyranny of religion and nationalism? Only the future (if there is one) will tell.

The 2000 Message

The end of 2000 marked the sixth anniversary of the Mark Twain Scholarship Fund and, of course, the end of the most remarkable century for humankind. Never before in the history of our species have we witnessed so many discoveries and innovations as those of the twentieth century.

Einstein's relativity, quantum mechanics, and the latest theory of chaos provided us with tools to unravel some of the complexities of our universe and escape the dogmatic beliefs of religion which for centuries have hampered the progress of science and stifled the mind of humankind. The prophetic stories of my favorite childhood author, Jules Verne, became a reality, and space became the new frontier.

The twentieth century was the era of social revolution as well. The institution of racial segregation, at least in most of the developed countries, was abolished, and the women's liberation movement, which had started in the nineteenth century, culminated in universal suffrage.

For the above reasons, and the despicable conditions for women still prevailing in Afghanistan and other third world countries, the selected topic for the 2000 essay competition was:

It has been recognized that humankind will thrive when the equality in all the fields of human endeavor between the sexes reaches its apogee. What are the obstacles to achieving this goal, and what should your generation do to eliminate them?

As we venture now into the dawn of the new millennium, you, the sponsors of our scholarship, are the change-makers of our time on the frontier of a new era.

The 1999 Message

As we approach the dawn of a new century and millennium, humankind is still plagued by antiquated ideas and superstitions despite the incredible advances of science and technology. Regional conflicts around the globe fuelled by religious or nationalistic sentiments are scarring our Earth's fragile environment. Also, the ever-increasing population explosion threatens our species and others with a premature and deplorable extinction.

Close to home, science education, which is the cornerstone of progress and understanding of our cosmos, is under attack by zealots whose religious beliefs are in conflict with evolution and the Big Bang cosmology. Notwithstanding the scientific evidence that unequivocally indicates that sexuality is encoded in our genes, the same religious fanatics continue to harass our gay and lesbian citizens.

Racial tension, although somewhat reduced, is by no means eliminated. Thus, the ugly head of racism continues to appear, spewing its repugnant venom. Finally, the continuous encroachment of religion on our government has eroded Jefferson's wall of separation of state and church, which can very much transform our constitutionally governed democracy into a totalitarian theocracy if not curtailed.

Can our country and humankind escape the march of folly and charter a new path toward enlightenment and hope for all in the new millennium? H. G. Wells once stated:

Human history becomes more and more a race between education and catastrophe.

Well aware of the profound challenges facing the new century, the trustees of the Mark Twain Scholarship Fund are more than ever dedicated to the advancement of intellectual thought. The scholarship will continue on its path guided by Mark Twain's conviction that the key to solving our problems is **education.**

For the above reason, the selected topic for the 1999 essay competition was:

Breaking the chains of the past to liberate the future.

The 1998 Message

As humankind prepares to venture into the third millennium, we at the Mark Twain Scholarship Fund are convinced more than ever before of the profound importance of education not only for a person's well-balanced life, but for the survival of our species. Humans have had a strong effect on their local environment, but only in the last century has the explosion of science and its by-product, technology, expanded this influence on a global scale. Our activities have already caused changes in the Earth's atmosphere, the land, the oceans, and the biosphere in general.

With these thoughts in mind, the trustees of the Mark Twain Scholarship Fund have committed themselves to the task of combating this destructive trend of humankind through education for the past five years.

Although the battle is beyond our present capabilities, we adhere to our motto:

It Is Better to Light a Candle Than to Curse the Darkness.

Dedicated to the advancement of intellectual thought, the scholarship will continue on its path guided by Mark Twain's conviction that:

The answer to all world problems is found in one word. The word is education

During the ten years of operation of the Mark Twain Scholarship, I did all the administrative work. Nevertheless, I enjoyed reading the submitted essays and the letters of appreciation from the young students who dared to apply to a scholarship sponsored by an atheist organization. I was especially gratified by the thank-you notes from the student recipients.

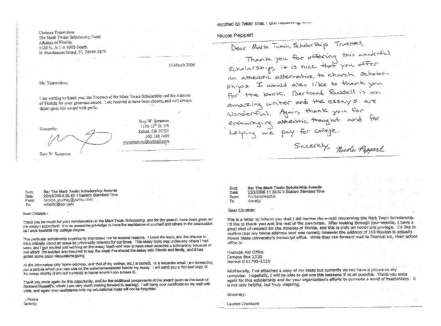

During my years of activism for civil rights, against war, and for the separation of state and church, I became known not only in Florida where I was a resident, but nationwide. I was interviewed by many newspaper reporters from Florida and other states as far as California. I was also invited by television and radio stations, including National Public Radio, in response to my state-church cases, letters to the editors, and lawsuits.

In 1987, when Pope John Paul II visited Miami and the United States, the city of Miami, the state of Florida, and the federal government spent about 3.5 million dollars to accommodate this religious leader. As chapter director of American Atheists, I joined with representatives of ACLU, other concerned citizens, and organizations in protest of this unconstitutional expenditure on the pope's arrival. The story has an amusing end.

When all the others, including the ACLU, backed out, I drafted a complaint with assistance from a chapter member who was a law student and filed a lawsuit in the United States District Court, Southern District of Florida, Case No. 87-1501-CIV—Kehoe. When I went to the court and filed the case with the clerk, I left a list of names to be called as witnesses. Among the names was the Catholic archbishop, who had sent a letter to the school board requesting that schools be closed so students could participate in the pope's celebration.

On the day of the trial, I went to court expecting to see all the witnesses. When I asked the judge about them, Judge Kehoe informed me that providing the names was not enough. I was supposed to have the witnesses subpoenaed, which I, not being a lawyer, had failed to do.

Infuriated with American Atheists for not providing me with an attorney, I proceeded to argue the case myself. With my limited knowledge of the law and my broken English at the time, I called to the witness stand the superintendent of the school board, the chief of police, and some others that were present and cross-examined them for about three hours.

In my closing arguments, I had the opportunity to make a statement.

> Your Honor (Judge Kehoe), as I stated before, I am not the right speaker to express what I feel correctly in English, but I will try my best.
>
> It is beyond any doubt to me, that the school board, the Dade County, the federal government, all the agencies that are working on this event are violating our First Amendment and they broke the wall of separation between state and church.
>
> The last few days we heard from a lot of sources about the significance and the historic event, but what is historic or what is going to become a historic event is not the visit of John Paul II on September 11th, but your decision today.
>
> History caught up with you personally, because you have to decide and preserve our Constitution, the integrity of this country and humanity's.

John Paul II is a religious leader and in the eyes of his followers is their holy father and the representative of a, and I quote, 'God.' In the name of this God, wars were waged, thousands of people were maimed and killed, the human mind was stifled and progress was hampered through the centuries. Because of this idea of God, our civilization suffered through the Dark Ages and is still suffering. Religion brought no good to humanity but harm and division. The wars that we have today in Iraq-Iran is a religious war, because their holy man Ayatollah Khomeini is also like John Paul II and he believes in his convictions. Yet, he sends twelve-year old boys to explode the mines so that tanks can pass safely after that.

I am sure, Your Honor, you know from your schooling what the history of humanity teaches. What religion did in this country and in Europe. In this country only one hundred years ago we burned witches in Salem because of religion. In Europe, on St. Bartholomew's Day more than 100,000 Protestants were slaughtered by the pope's people. By the Catholics.

Science suffered because of religion. Galileo was confined to his home until he died, and Copernicus escaped with his life because he was lucky to get away.

Others though like Giordano Bruno did not escape. He was burned at the stake. His burning was not conducted in a way that put him to rest easy, but they used to place the fire close enough and yet far enough so that the victim suffered more. They belied that by suffering his '[soul' will be saved.

This is what religion gave us, Your Honor.

Today our planet is in the greatest danger. We are threatened by population explosion. We humans, because religion gave us the idea that we are something extra special, a special creation of this imaginary 'God,' have dominated the whole planet, we extinct thousands of other species, and we are doing everything possible to bring total disaster.

Yet this particular religious leader, John Paul II, with his moral directives forbidding the use of birth control with contraceptives, even if there is a danger to contract a deadly disease like AIDS, is not advancing the good of civilization. He is harming the whole human species. And not only the human species, but also the other species on this planet as well.

It is appalling that the school board, Dade County, and even the federal government violated our Constitution and crumbled the wall of separation our wise founders established in this country.

I travelled all over the world, Your Honor, and I visited different countries studying their customs and religions. I found no other country on this planet with a Constitution like ours with a separation of state and church. So, as I said before, history caught up with you and you have to make this historic decision to uphold the Constitution and the First Amendment.

Thank you very much.

Me in front of Bruno's statue in Rome at the plaza where he was burned alive.

I lost the case on technicalities. Again, the media had a field day. After the trial, the local newspapers interviewed me and published long articles. In the following days our home phone rang every few minutes with vitriolic threats by the good Catholics. We had to change our phone to a new unlisted number.

Atheist says pope spending violates Constitution

Atheists don't believe pope trip worth the cost

JOHN PAUL'S VISIT

JOHN PAUL'S VISIT

Christos Tzanetakos says it's not the pope's visit itself that upsets him, only the use of tax money to accommodate it.

By TIM O'MEILIA
Palm Beach Post Staff Writer

Christos Tzanetakos, an ardent atheist, says he doesn't mind that half a million people will stand on tiptoe along Biscayne Boulevard to greet Pope John Paul II in Miami Sept. 10.

"Some of my friends are Christians," he says.

Nor does he mind that another 250,000 or more will rub shoulders at Tamiami Park the next morning to hear the pope say Mass.

"We tolerate anyone's religious views, exactly because we are atheists," said the Miami resident. "If they want to believe in the Holy Ghost, fine."

Just don't ask him to pay for what he regards as religious celebrations.

About $3 million in state and local money will be spent on the pope's 23½-hour stopover, and the Archdiocese of Miami and surrounding dioceses will spend $2 million. Tzanetakos doesn't like it.

"Jesus gave his speech on a mountain," Tzanetakos said. "We have no objection to the pope going to the Everglades to give his speech, where he won't create havoc in Miami by closing the schools, clogging the roads and involving 70 percent of the police force in his protection, leaving the rest of the city vulnerable."

Spending tax money to welcome the pope is a clear violation of the constitutional separation of church and state, Tzanetakos and his 40-member chapter of American Atheists believe.

"We feel it's not only unconstitutional and offensive, it's criminal

ATHEISTS/from 1A

for American government officials to welcome the leader of the church which persecuted Galileo and Kepler. Religion is the most tremendous force that divides humanity on this planet."

Church officials take a different view. Monsignor Jude O'Doherty, head of the archdiocese's papal visit committee, said the pope was "both a head of state and the head of a religion."

"Spending money to protect a foreign head of state and to welcome him is certainly appropriate," O'Doherty said.

Tzanetakos has at least the moral support of the Society of Separationists, the group founded by outspoken atheist Madalyn Murray O'Hair. "Some people claim it's a historical event, that the religious aspect is secondary to its historical nature," said John Vinson, attorney for the Austin, Texas-based society. "We don't go for that."

Tzanetakos and his chapter also is miffed that:

■ No classes will be held in Dade County public schools the day of the Mass. The Dade County School Board has designated Sept. 11 as a teacher planning day.

■ The School Board had planned to lend 600 idle school buses to Dade County to lend to the Archdiocese of Miami to transport worshippers. That plan was scrapped when the county refused to accept liability for the buses.

■ Criminal trials are being postponed that week so police will be free to provide security.

■ Two weeks before the visit, a 90-foot cross was to be erected at Florida International University as a backdrop to the pope's outdoor Mass.

Although he is a member of a committee formed by the American Civil Liberties Union to oversee public spending for the visit, Tzanetakos is not happy with the results.

"The ACLU is trying to compromise," he said. "They're not trying to defend the constitution."

Another case that I won and infuriated all the Christians in the state of Florida was the revision of the notary public oath.

In 1990, I applied to become a notary in the State of Florida. When I received the application form with the oath ending with the phrase, "So help me God," I sent a letter to the Secretary of State, Jim Smith, requesting the removal of this phrase as unconstitutional. The State agreed, and to the chagrin of the Christians in Florida, "So help me God" was removed. Thus I became a notary public, taking the oath without the God reference.

FLORIDA DEPARTMENT OF STATE

Jim Smith
Secretary of State

DIVISION OF ELECTIONS
Room 1801, The Capitol, Tallahassee, Florida 32399-0250
(904) 488-7690

February 13, 1990

Mr. Christos Tzanetakos
Director
South Florida Chapter of
   American Atheists
Post Office Box 660602
Miami Springs, Florida 33266-0602

Dear Mr. Tzanetakos:

The Secretary of State, Jim Smith, has referred your letter of January 29, 1990 to me.

We appreciate you bringing to our attention the court case Torcaso v. Watkins, 367 U.S. 488 (1961). 81 SCt 1680; 6 LEd 982

The Department of State is in the process of revising the notary forms, and we will remove the words "so help me God" from the notary oath. This new form will be effective February 28, 1990.

Sincerely,

Phyllis Slater
Assistant General Counsel

Again, the media had a field day.

SOUTH BROWARD FINAL

Saturday, February 17, 1990   25 cents

State striking 'God' from oath
Wording on notary form antiquated, government says

By LYDA LONGA
Staff Writer

Notaries no longer will be forced by the state to seek divine intervention.

The words "so help me God" are being stricken from their written oath of office because of complaints from a South Florida atheist who said the clause violates the separation of church and state.

"Those words never should have been there to begin with," Ken Rouse, general counsel for the Florida Department of State, said on Friday. "The wording on some of these forms is sometimes antiquated."

Rouse said he did not know whether the forms for other state offices would be changed because it was unclear whether others include the clause.

The challenge to the wording was brought by Christos Tzanetakos, director of the South Florida Chapter of American Atheists.

Tzanetakos, 52, of North Miami, said he was outraged when he applied to become a notary last month and discovered the words "so help me God" on the oath's affirmation form.

In an angry letter to the state, Tzanetakos pointed out that the courts had ruled that such oaths were unconstitutional. The state agreed.

"It was just an oversight on the state's part to leave those words on the oath over all these years, and it took this gentleman to point that out to us," Rouse said.

SEE OATH /7A

FROM PAGE 1A
State to remove 'so help me God' from notary form

Religious leaders from Miami to Jacksonville were shocked.

"This is frightening, that one person could sway the state to change things like that," said Glen Owens, assistant executive director of the Florida Baptist Convention in Jacksonville. "How can they completely abolish a system of doing things for one person?"

The Rev. Gerard LaCerra, chancellor of the Archdiocese of Miami, was equally surprised.

"What are we supposed to base our commitments on if something like this is removed?" he asked. "The state?"

The Rev. Robin Tripp, assistant pastor of Fifth Avenue Church of God in Deerfield Beach, also was upset by the change in the oath.

"There has to be something that a man can swear by," Tripp said. "I'm afraid that if you take these words away, the oath will not be as strong and people may not trust the man that swears by it because there are no standards."

But Tzanetakos, an engineer who began to doubt the strict religious teachings of his Greek Orthodox parents when he was 16, said the issue is not whether you believe in God, but whether the state can force you to swear to a deity.

"This change is a first step in the separation of church and state," Tzanetakos said from his home on Friday. "We have come a long way from the 1940s and 1950s with the McCarthy era.

"There is hope yet."

During my long years of activism, I had more challenges regarding state-church separation.

When our daughter was attending the University of Florida in Gainesville, Alice and I went to visit her and stayed in the campus hotel. I noticed a copy of the Christian Bible in the nightstand. Since the hotel is part of the State University, I sent a letter to the hotel manager and demanded the removal of the Bibles. Soon they were removed from all the rooms.

I was also instrumental in establishing a Florida ordinance forbidding the erection of religious icons (crosses or shrines) at the side of highways where people were killed in auto accidents. The crosses were replaced with a secular sign approved by the State.

An atheist's crusade for church, state separation

Christos Tzanetakos of Atheists of Florida.

By RON HAYES
Palm Beach Post Staff Writer

Christos Tzanetakos is a born-again atheist.

"We are all *born* atheists," he explains with a patient smile. "Nobody is born with any religion."

Take a child born to Christian parents, he reasons, raise the child in a Muslim household, and that child will be Muslim. Take the infant daughter of Jews, raise her Catholic, and Catholic she will be.

"Religion is an inherited trait,"

he says.

Born in Greece 58 years ago, Tzanetakos was brought up Greek Orthodox. In high school, a fascination with physics moved him to question the Bible's inconsistencies.

"The book of Genesis says that God created the light on the first day, then on the fourth day he created the sun and moon. Well, now we know that light comes

Please see ATHEIST/4D

ATHEIST
From 1D

from the sun, so how could there have been light before there was the sun?" he wondered.

Later, traveling the world as a merchant seaman, he read philosophy and studied the world's great religions. As a Miami marine engineer, he became active in the atheist movement.

Born atheist, raised Greek Orthodox, born-again atheist.

Today, as president of Atheists of Florida, Inc., Tzanetakos oversees the 300-member organization from a retirement condo in Fort Pierce, which he shares with Alice, his wife of 25 years. His recent crusade to remove the personalized roadside "shrines" erected in memory of drunk-driving victims is a success, but only the latest in a decade of battles to guard the Constitution's separation of church and state with — well, almost religious zeal:

■ In 1987, Tzanetakos, who is not a lawyer, argued before a federal judge in Miami to block the closing of public schools during Pope John Paul II's visit to the city. He lost, then condemned the $3 million in public money spent to host the pontiff.

■ A year later, he complained the Lord's Prayer was being recited during Alcoholics Anonymous meetings at a Dade County drug treatment center. That effort failed under a Supreme Court ruling that religious meetings in public buildings are constitutional as long as no public money is spent on the group and the primary purpose — helping alcoholics — is secular.

■ In 1990, he demanded the removal of a 2-ton statue of Christ submerged under 20 feet of water and more than 3 miles offshore in John Pennekamp Coral Reef State Park. The statue remains, but that same year he persuaded the state to drop " . . . so help me God" from the written oath to become a notary public.

■ In 1991, the University of Florida agreed to remove Bibles from 36 guest rooms of an on-campus hotel after he complained.

Even civil libertarians sympathetic to his First Amendment absolutism might wonder if Tzanetakos doesn't weaken his own cause when he objects to a religious symbol you'd need a boat and snorkeling gear to chance on.

"Well, you can forget the statue of Christ in the park," he answers, unswayed. "But if you forget the small thing, which is insignificant, then you go from a small to another one to another. It's a matter of principle."

In 1991, principle moved Tzanetakos to split from American Atheists, the national organization founded by Madalyn Murray O'Hair, the combative atheist whose landmark 1963 suit ended in a Supreme Court ban on organized prayer in public schools. Tzanetakos had been a board member of that group's Miami chapter, but left to help form the independent Atheists of Florida, Inc.

"Madalyn O'Hair and her family did not like it when I suggested we have elections for officers instead of them being appointed by her," he says. "Atheists of Florida is totally democratic."

Tzanetakos and O'Hair also differ hugely in style. O'Hair, who mysteriously dropped from sight in September 1995, always seemed to relish the contempt she holds for people who believe in God. Tzanetakos is quick to emphasize that he offers religious people the same tolerance he asks in return.

"Atheists, as a rule, are not anti-religion," he says. "The philosophy of atheism is toleration. We are on one planet, one boat, and we have to cooperate."

That spirit of cooperation has manifested itself in ways that might surprise those who imagine atheists as snarling curmudgeons full of contempt and devoid of charity.

My favorite subject as a student and in later years was physics. Albert Einstein and Richard P. Feynman were my most admired physicists and philosophers.

When I was invited by the Forum Club in Hollywood, Florida, to speak in one of their meetings, I delivered a speech on Einstein and his famous equation $E=mc^2$

Following is my presentation.

$E=mc^2$: Its Meaning and Its Consequences

Einstein's $E=mc^2$, the most important and undoubtedly the profoundest equation in humankind's history, is perhaps the most universally known equation. Unfortunately, most of the people outside the scientific communities have not the foggiest idea as to the meaning of the equation. The average person associates Einstein and his formula mostly with the development of the nuclear bomb. Therefore, let us examine the equation in terms that can be understood by all. 'E' of course stands for 'energy,' 'm' stands for 'mass' and 'c' stands for the 'speed of light.'

$E=mc^2$ is the fundamental equation in the special theory of relativity that tells us that energy and matter can be converted from one to the other. Consequently, Einstein was the first genius to realize that energy and matter are actually different facets of the same essence. Now, let us go back to the equation $E=mc^2$ and examine its components.

Energy

Back in the 1950s, my high school text of physics defined energy as the ability or capacity to do work (we will come back to the definition of energy). There are several forms of energy, including heat, chemical, electrical, and so forth, all of which fall into two broad energy categories, namely potential (or stored) energy and kinetic (or motion) energy. Energy (or its equivalent matter) can be neither created nor destroyed (this is the law of conservation of matter and energy). However, it can be changed from one form into another. Again, we will expand on this farther down in our discourse.

Mass

Mass (symbolized by *m*) is the property of matter that resists the acceleration to an applied force. Mass can also be defined as proportional to the weight of a body in a gravitational field. In the international system the standard unit of mass is the kilogram (kg).

Mass is not the same thing as weight. Weight on Earth is the force exerted between the Earth and any object. On the Earth's surface, an object's weight is its mass x the Earth's gravitational acceleration. Or weight = mg, where m=its mass and g=9.81 m/s².

Therefore the weight of one kilogram mass would be =1kg.9.8 m/s². = 9.81 N (Newton)

However, an object weighing one kilogram or 2.2 pounds on Earth would weigh only about 0.36 kg or 0.8 pounds on Mars. On Jupiter it would weigh roughly 2.5 kgs or 5.5 pounds. In other gravitational settings it will weigh according to the prevailing gravitational force (the masses of the objects and the distance between their centers).

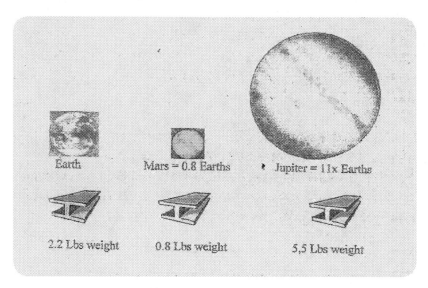

Earth   Mars = 0.8 Earths   Jupiter = 11x Earths

2.2 Lbs weight   0.8 Lbs weight   5,5 Lbs weight

Speed of Light

The speed of light is approximately 186,282.397 miles per second, or in metric units, *c* equals 299792458 meters per second or, rounded, 300,000,000 meters/sec. For our theoretical calculations we must convert the speed from meters to centimeters, which is 300,000,000x100 (a meter, of course, has 100 centimeters).

If we now apply the above rounded speed of light to the equation $E=mc^2$, we would have:

$$E=m.(300,000,000 \times 100)^2 \text{ or } E=m.9.10^{20}$$

9.10^{20} now is a very large number (900000000000000000000).

Therefore, even a small amount of matter (mass) when converted into energy can be devastating as in the case of a nuclear bomb.

The conversion of matter into energy on our planet occurred naturally by the decay of radioactive materials, a process that still continues. With the advent of Einstein's equation, scientists achieved the means for the transformation or conversion of matter into energy by splitting the atom or by fusing atoms.

In both cases, in fission or fusion, the by-products have less mass than the original. For example, when we fuse one deuterium (a heavy hydrogen isotope) with one tritium (another even heavier hydrogen isotope), we get a new atom of helium, a neutron and energy.

Deuterium + Tritium> Helium + Neutron + Energy

Now, the weight (mass) of Deuterium is: 2,0147
and that of Tritium is: 3,0170
The sum of the two is: 5,0317

The by-products of the above fusion are:
Helium with an atomic weight of 4,0038
and neutron with a weight of: 1,0089 + (Energy)
The sum of the byproducts is: 5,0127

The difference between the fusing parts and the by-products is:
5,0317-5,0127 = 0,0190

We call this 'mass deficit,' and it is this deficit of mass that is transformed into energy.

Again, this is a very small amount of mass (matter), but when this is multiplied by the square speed of light the amount of energy is very large. The energy then released from the fusion of one deuterium and one tritium is:

$$E = 0.019 \times 9 \times 10^{20}$$

The above can be better understood by the following depiction of the fusion process where the scale of the fusing parts is heavier than the by-products.

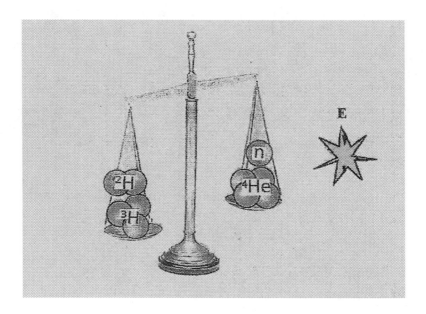

In today's nuclear reactors, the energy is used to serve humankind's ever increasing needs for electricity. For example, if we could convert, say, a kilogram (2.2 pounds) of coal, the equivalent electrical energy would be 25 billion kilowatt hours of electricity. This is enough energy to meet the residential, industrial, and commercial needs of New York City for more than two months. Therefore, the peaceful exploration of fusion energy can free humankind from the pollution of conventional means of energy production such as coal and petroleum.

It will also eliminate the dangers associated with the harmful radiation from the current fission nuclear reactors or future catastrophic meltdowns such as the Chernobyl accident of 26 April, 1986, when at 1:23:44, the reactor in unit no. 4 ran out of control and exploded.

Unfortunately, the first application of the fruits of $E=mc^2$ was the creation of the atom and hydrogen bombs. The bombings of Hiroshima and Nagasaki took place on August 6, 1945, and August 9, 1945, respectively. In a matter of seconds, over 200,000 Japanese men, women, and children were annihilated. The majority of the survivors suffered the effects of radiation that later produced leukemia and other forms of cancer.

The justification for the Hiroshima and Nagasaki bombings is that they ended the war months sooner, saving many lives on both sides. However, the war was almost over, and the Japanese had by then been covertly seeking an end to hostilities. That the bombings expedited the end of the war is nothing but a poor excuse for the guilty conscience of the American victors.

Hiroshima and Nagasaki will go down in history as the vilest crime of humankind and the darkest page in the history of the United States of America.

The skeleton of the Gembakou observatory after the bomb

Today Hiroshima and Nagasaki have been rebuilt, and only the naked dome and the skeleton of the Gembakou observatory has been left standing as it was found after the explosion. It stands there to remind humankind of the insanity of war and the cruelty of warmongers.

Ironically, the monument is dedicated as a "peace monument," which in my opinion is the ultimate oxymoron. Perhaps the best dedication would be: "Monument to the Cruelty of Man"

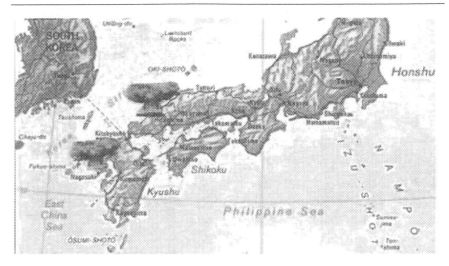

Did we learn from Hiroshima and Nagasaki?

Despite the efforts of Albert Einstein, Bertrand Russell, the great antiwar activist, philosopher, and mathematician, and many other scientists who advocated the nonproliferation of nuclear weapons, our planet has become a keg of nuclear, chemical, and bacteriological explosives of mass destruction, waiting to be ignited by any lunatic who might gain control of the button. Sadly, our country has the largest stockpiles of the above-mentioned agents of death and destruction.

In particular, did we, the Americans, learn from the past?

Since World War II, our foreign policies supporting cruel dictators and corrupt governments around the globe have directly or indirectly caused the most despicable acts of human cruelties, culminating with the present state of terror on our planet.

Well, let us close this shameful and sad chapter of history and return to the $E=mc^2$ and examine the deeper meaning and its consequences. As I stated earlier, the splitting of the atom and the fusion of hydrogen into helium verified Einstein's claim that the universe is composed by one essence that manifests itself in the dual form of matter and energy. It is precisely this realization that makes $E=mc^2$ so profound.

Astronomer Edwin Hubble discovered that the galaxies in the known universe are receding from each other causing the expansion of the universe. As a consequence, astrophysicist George Gamow conceived the idea of the Big Bang theory. George Gamow reasoned that if the galaxies are moving away from each other, then it had to be a time when they were all concentrated in one place. (This in cosmology is now known as the singularity).

The essence of the universe in this state was pure energy of unimaginable density and heat. Then according to Gamow and his Big Bang theory, an explosion took place about thirteen billion years ago. When the expanding universe started to cool down, the universal essence of energy transformed itself into the present day combination of matter and energy.

And here is the deeper meaning of $E=mc^2$.

If the universe is made from energy, which according to the law of conservation cannot be created out of nothing and neither can be destroyed, it begs the question: whence, and why, and whither?

The journey of our quest to answer the above and understand our universe has taken us from the primitive mythological and religious explanations to the mind-boggling concepts of relativity, quantum mechanics, and nuclear physics. It brought us to the realization that the dawn of our universe broke more than thirteen billion years ago (13.7) from the elusive essence of energy as it existed at the state of the singularity.

And now I have to come back to the definition of energy as the capacity to do work. To me this definition is not clear and does not describe the elusive essence of the universe (energy). For example, carbon (a physical entity, matter) has the *ability* or *capacity* to unite its atoms in chains and rings of various configurations. Also, it has the *capacity* or *ability* to unite with the atoms of other elements.

Therefore, is it appropriate to define carbon as the *ability* or *capacity* to form chains, rings, or to unite with other elements?

Of course, the above definition of carbon will be considered as illogical. Similarly, energy (a physical entity, or actually the only universal entity or essence at the state of singularity) to be defined by its ability (a quality with no physical substance) to do work in my opinion is inappropriate.

Personally, if I had to define energy, I would say:

Energy is the elusive universal essence which contains all the forces of nature (gravitational force, electromagnetic force, strong and weak force).

Then we can still state that $E=mc^2$ or that the work of energy when its force is applied on a body is:

Work = force times the distance through which the force acts on the body (Kinetic Energy). Or $F=ma$ (force equals mass times acceleration).

In his book *Cosmos*, Carl Sagan wrote:

'In many cultures it is customary to answer that God created the universe out of nothing. But this is mere temporizing. If we wish courageously to pursue the question, we must, of course ask next where God comes from. And if we decide this to be unanswerable, why not save a step and decide that the origin of the universe is an unanswerable question? Or, if we say that God has always existed, why not save a step and conclude that the universe has always existed?'

For me though, the pseudoscientific idea of a god who gave birth to all religions and that, along with the other impostor, nationalism, has been responsible for the worst calamities on our planet and most probably will be the reason for our premature extinction, is total paranoia.

An example for the above argument can be made from the idea of the physical numbers. In numbers we have the positive numbers starting from zero to infinity, and the negative numbers starting again from zero to infinity.

Infinity . . . . -7, -6, -5, -4, -3, -2, -1, 0 +1, +2, +3, +4, +5, +6, +7 . . . Infinity

Similar to the physical numbers, in nature everything comes in opposites. For every particle there is an antiparticle. For someone to claim that a number beyond infinity created the numbers is equally absurd with the idea of an entity beyond the natural universe, a god, who created the universe out of nothing. Therefore, the only good thing that I can say about the idea of god is that which George Bernard Shaw humorously stated:

I'm an atheist and I thank God for it

Christos Tzanetakos
Founder, Atheists of Florida, Inc.
Member, American Association for the Advancement of Science

Sources:
1. Angelos Kordoulis, "Nuclear Energy-Nuclear Bomb"
2. Albert Einstein, *Ideas and Opinions*
3. Carl Sagan, *Cosmos*
4. Lincoln Barnett, *The Universe and Dr. Einstein*
5. Murphy, Hollon, Zitzewitz, Smoot, "Physics"
6. Donald Goldsmith, *The Evolving Universe*
7. Philip James Edwin Peebles, *Principles of Physical Cosmology*
8. Wikipedia

In 1999 I was invited by students of the Embry-Riddle Aeronautical University at Daytona Beach, Florida, to give them a speech. My speech was titled:

Life: A Phenomenon of Organized Complexity
What is Life or Living Matter?

In the next twenty minutes or so, I would like to take you on an imaginary voyage back in time and space and try to unravel the phenomenon we call life.

Our planet Earth, which in size is not even a mote in the stellar universe, is made up, like the rest of the cosmos, of the same universal essence that manifests itself in the dual form of matter or energy.

As far as we know, life exists only on our small planet. Of course, the universe might be, and most probably is, brimming with life, but as of now, we have no verifiable evidence proving our assumptions.

At this point I would like to mention that a group of researchers strongly advocates the hypothesis that life may have been seeded from space by comets, meteorites, or interplanetary dust that shuttled the first organic molecules from which life on our planet evolved. But no matter if this notion is valid or invalid; the question still remains.

Well then, we might ask, how did life or the first living molecule or living matter originate?

Stuart Kauffman, a biologist and mathematician, experimented with 'Boolean networks' after George Boole, an English mathematician, and I would like to quote from Roger Lewin's book *Complexity*.

> The network proceeds through a series of so-called states. At a given instant, each element in the network examines the signals arriving from the links with other elements, and then is active or inactive, according to its rules for reacting to the signals.
>
> The network then proceeds to the next state, whereupon the process repeats itself. And so on, and so on.
>
> Under certain circumstances a network may proceed through all its possible states before repeating any one of them. In practice, however, the network at some point hits a series of states around which it cycles repeatedly.

While Stuart Kauffman experimented with computers, Stanley Miller and Harold Urey back in 1953 subjected a mixture of gases, similar to the ones prevailing in the prebiotic Earth, to electrical charges. Out of the inorganic gases they discovered the formation of organic compounds.

And so, similar to the Boolean networks, the approximately 100 physical elements whose combinations can be astronomical hit upon a particular state, and the new network has been repeating itself ever since, setting in motion the phenomenon of a new dance we call life.

At this point a religious person or even a nonreligious one might ask: well, how did these elements and the electric charges (energy) come into being? There must be a master designer who designed and programmed the whole picture. This is a very valid and rational question.

The answer to this comes from **physics**, and in particular **thermodynamics,** which states that matter or energy cannot be created out of nothing, nor can it be destroyed. Therefore, the essence of the universe (matter or energy) has neither a beginning nor an end. Consequently, the universe **does not need a creator**. If, on the other hand, we do accept the existence of a supernatural power, a 'god,' an oxymoron in itself, the question still remains, from where did this god come?

What happened after the formation of the first primordial living matter and the advent of the first living molecule by the almighty **chance** is easy to understand if we reflect on the development of our own species.

The first molecules like our first ancestors (the species *Homo sapiens*) can be traced back to the approximate time of their origin. Of course, the exact date of their origin is rather irrelevant for our train of thought. Let us go then to when the first couple of our species appeared and formed the first family. Their occupation, we can assume, was to search for food and therefore, we can call them the 'food searchers' (hunters, gatherers). Eventually, other families joined (don't ask where they came from) as it is again irrelevant, and thus formed small bands or tribes.

We can again assume that at some point an ancestor discovered how to make a pair of shoes, for example, to protect his or her feet. Other members of the tribe requested shoes for themselves and here we have a new occupation a 'shoemaker.' From then on, when our ancestors moved from families to tribes, city states, state unions, union of nations, etc. and with the explosion of science and technology, the various types of occupations increased exponentially. You can get a good picture of the complexity of the modern world if you open a telephone directory in a big city like New York, where millions of specialized individuals are working in unison, and the whole city can be considered as a unit. (This is a very important point.) Similarly, settlements, villages, cities, and states interact in unison to create a larger unit like our country.

Furthermore, former independent countries formed new unions, like the European Union. Hopefully, we will form an even larger union to include all the inhabitants of our planet before we annihilate our species and those who might perish with us in the event of a man-made catastrophe.

How did our species achieve this tremendous progress from the primitive stage to the sophistication of our stellar exploration era?

The answer, of course, is well known and understood. We surpassed the other species not because we are **endowed** with or **destined** by a creator, but rather because we developed the ability to pass the knowledge of one generation to the next through the medium of the spoken and written language.

Well, expanding on the human species, we forgot our primordial cell, or let us call it our primordial gene. Let us go back then and compare the first living molecules with the members of our species. Like our ancestors who became shoemakers, mechanics, doctors, judges, teachers, counseling psychologists, computer programmers, philosophers, etc., working in unison to form villages, cities, states, and countries, the living molecules achieved this very complex task in every living entity, whether a human, other animal, plant, or insect. Similarly, we can ask how the living molecules learned to perform the various tasks and from a simple amoebae type organism evolved into the complex life forms of today. The answer again is language.

For a long time, the ancient language of hieroglyphics remained a mystery and gave the early anthropologists and archaeologists many headaches and sleepless nights. As you know, their predicament was ended with the discovery of the Rosetta Stone, whose inscription of a text in the two languages of hieroglyphics and Greek solved their problem.

Well, similar to the Rosetta Stone, the discovery of DNA by Francis Crick and James D. Watson unmasked the mystery of the language of life. We now know that all life forms pass their information or genetic instructions from one generation to the next using the same universal language whose alphabet consists of only four letters: A, G, C, and T. Of course, in reality, the letters AGCT are only symbols representing four chemical bases; therefore, the language of life is chemical in nature. With the discovery of DNA and the study of the genetic code of different species, we can now proudly claim the monkeys as our close cousins.

Related to this discourse, I would like to quote from Richard Dawkins's latest book *River Out of Eden*.

> The 'paragraph' in our genes describing the protein called cytochrome c is 339 letters long. Twelve letter changes separate human cytochrome c from the cytochrome c of horses, our rather distant cousins.

Only one cytochrome c letter change separates humans from monkeys (our fairly close cousins), one letter change separates horses from donkeys (their very close cousins) and three letter changes separate horses from pigs (their somewhat more distant cousins).

Forty-five letter changes separate humans from yeast and the same number separates pigs from yeast.

Right now, hundreds of scientists around the globe are feverishly working to translate the instruction books of the species. The project known as The Human Genome has already revealed how the various specialized cells in our bodies learn to perform their various tasks.

The new knowledge has profound and invaluable implications for the study of genetically transmitted diseases. One of the most recent achievements directly connected to the Human Genome Project was the creation of a human ear on the back of a mouse, which was then transplanted to a human recipient. Ironically, on May18, 1995, a group of about 200 religious leaders issued the following statement:

> We, the undersigned religious leaders, oppose the patenting of human and animal life forms.
>
> We are disturbed by the US Patent Office's recent decision to patent human body parts and several genetically engineered animals.
>
> We believe that humans and animals are creations of God, not humans, and as such should not be patented as human inventions.

Of course, the difference with a scientist or an atheist is the acceptance that we are the outcome of the first primordial cell created by chance. Naturally, this view is vehemently opposed by religious leaders, who are still invoking Paley's argument of design.

In *Natural Theology*, William Paley (1802) compares the eye with a human designed instrument as the telescope, and concludes that 'There is precisely the same proof that the eye was made for vision, as there is that the telescope was made for assisting it.' Therefore, the eye must have a designer, just as the telescope had.

Perhaps we have to thank Paley for the above argument, because the comparison of the eye to the optical instrument can give us another striking example of life's emergence by blind chance to today's complexity through Darwinian evolution. Let us then explore the emergence and development (evolution) of our optical instrument from the very simple to the most complex such as the Hubble telescope. We can assume that the first step was to 'create' the basic material for optical instruments, which is glass.

In the beginning there was no glass:

> And the earth was without form, and void, and darkness was upon the face of the deep.

That is to say, in the beginning there was no glass until one day a caravan of Arabs set up camp on a desert. The cook, knowing that there are no stones in a desert, had brought along with hardwood some limestone to build a fireplace.

And here we have by **chance** the three ingredients of glass (silica or sand, lime, and soda from the ashes of hardwood). You can imagine the astonishment of our cook, when the morning after, he discovered the first piece of glass.

Well, from then on, we can trace the evolution of our optical instruments from the very simple to the most complex radio telescope of today as it is illustrated by the pictures 1 through 4.

Picture 1.	Picture 2.	Picture 3.	Picture 4.
A simple lens	Reflecting telescope	The large array	Hubble

Similarly, the emergence of life and its evolution originated by chance and followed the same evolutionary pattern.

Let us then examine the emergence and evolution of life on our planet.

As we can see from chart 1, the formation of planet Earth took place approximately four and a half billion years ago. Also, to give a comparison of the different stages in geological terms, let us assume that this was accomplished on January 1 (see chart 1). For about 1.15 billion years our planet was devoid of life until the elements in the primordial oceans, like the Boolean networks mentioned earlier, hit upon a particular state to form the building blocks of life (amino acids).

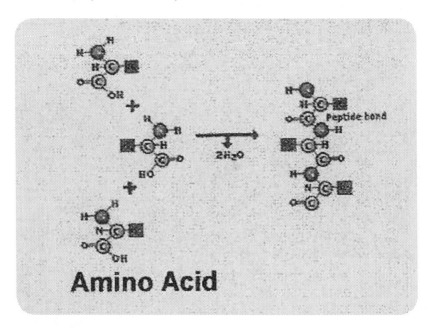

And thus 3.5 billion years ago, or on March 24, the first prokaryotic cells appeared.

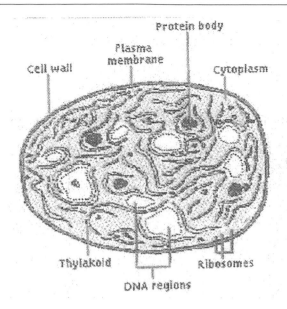

The prokaryotic cells divided and multiplied for two billion years before the more sophisticated eukaryotic cells made their appearance 1.5 billion years ago, or on September 3rd.

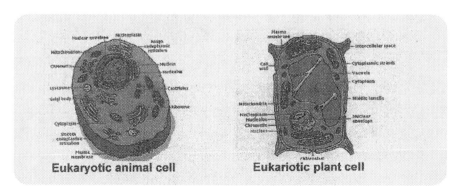

Eukaryotic animal cell   **Eukariotic plant cell**

From then on, algae appeared 700,000,000 years ago, or on November 3, shellfish and trilobites 570,000,000 years ago, or on November 15, fish 500,000,000 years ago, or on November 21, and reptiles 320,000,000 million years ago, or on December 5. It took another 95,000,000 million years before the dinosaurs and the first mammals made their appearance 225,000,000 million years ago or on December 12. Birds appeared 195,000,000 million years ago, or on December 15, and primates and flowering plants entered the arena 136,000,000 million years ago, or on December 19. Human beings appeared 2.5 million years ago, or on December 29 (as we can see, the segment on the chart is so infinitesimal that it cannot be shown). Similarly, the segment representing the current 10,000 years, which is the last minute before midnight of December 29, also cannot be presented on the chart.

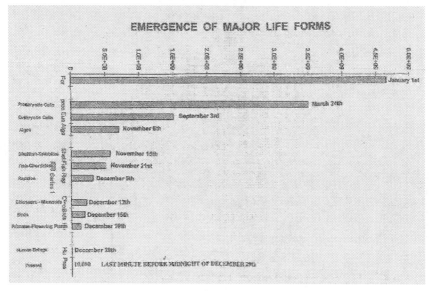

Chart 1

Reflecting on all the above, Nobel Laureate Richard Feynman very profoundly and eloquently stated this in his public speech to the National Academy of Sciences. I would like to quote part of his thoughts.

By the Sea
here it is
standing:
atoms with consciousness;
matter with curiosity.
stands at the sea,
wonders at wondering; I
a universe of atoms
an atom in the universe.

What then makes you and me and every living entity is the same living molecule, which through billions of years of evolution learned to perform different tasks in unison with other molecules and became the bone, muscle, tissue, hair, neuron, and so forth, of you and me.

In conclusion, life is a phenomenon of organized complexity. The designer of you, me, and 'every creeping thing that creepeth upon the earth,' is the same primordial gene that emerged by blind chance and is passing its instructions through the language of DNA to the coming generations of species.

Closing, I would like to quote Carl Sagan from his book *Cosmos*

> *The size and age of the Cosmos (Universe) are beyond ordinary human understanding. Lost somewhere between immensity and eternity is our tiny planetary home. In a cosmic perspective, most human concerns seem insignificant, even petty. And yet our species is young and curious and brave and shows much promise.*
>
> *In the last few millennia we have made the most astonishing and unexpected discoveries about the Cosmos and our place within it, explorations that are exhilarating to consider. They remind us that humans have evolved to wonder, that understanding is a joy, that knowledge is prerequisite to survival. I believe our future depends on how well we know this Cosmos in which we float like a mote of dust in the morning sky.*

Thank You

By: Christos Tzanetakos

Founder, Atheists of Florida, Inc.

Founder, The Mark Twain Scholarship Fund, Inc.

Member, American Association for the Advancement Of Science

Sources:

1. Stuart A. Kauffman, *The Origins of Order*
2. Roger Lewin, *Complexity*
3. Richard Dawkins, *River Out of Eden*
4. Francis Crick, *The Astonishing Hypothesis*

5. Richard P. Feynman, public speech at NAS
6. Microsoft Encarta 97 Encyclopedia
7. Carl Sagan, Cosmos

Richard Feynman is one of my most admired scientists and philosophers. I read his books and biography *Genius* by James Gleick, and I was impressed by the speech Richard P. Feynman delivered to the National Academy of Sciences entitled "The Value of Science."

I added illustrations to the speech and translated the text into Greek for my friends in Greece.

The Value of Science
RICHARD P. FEYNMAN

Selection of illustrations by: Christos Tzanetakos

Richard P. Feynman

Of all its many values, the greatest must be the freedom to doubt

From time to time, people suggest to me that scientists ought to give more consideration to social problems—especially that they should be more responsible in considering the impact of science upon society. This same suggestion must be made to many other scientists, and it seems to be generally believed that if the scientists would only look at these very difficult social problems and not spend so much time fooling with the less vital scientific ones, great success would come of it.

It seems to me that we do think about these problems from time to time, but we don't put full-time effort into them—the reason being that we know we don't have any magic formula for solving problems, that social problems are very much harder than scientific ones, and that we usually don't get anywhere when we do think about them.

I believe that a scientist looking at nonscientific problems is just as dumb as the next guy—and when he talks about a nonscientific matter, he will sound as naive as anyone untrained in the matter. Since the question of the value of science is not a scientific subject, this discussion is dedicated to proving my point—by example.

The first way in which science is of value is familiar to everyone. It is that scientific knowledge enables us to do all kinds of things and to make all kinds of things.

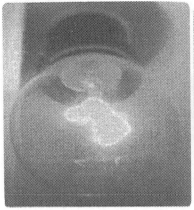 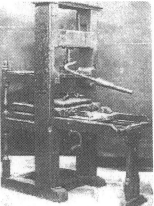

Electric light   The Gutenberg press

Of course if we make good things, it is not only to the credit of science; it is also to the credit of the moral choice which led us to good work. Scientific knowledge is an enabling power to do either good or bad—but it does not carry instructions on how to use it. Such power has evident value—even though the power may be negated by what one does.

I learned a way of expressing this common human problem on a trip to Honolulu. In a Buddhist temple there, the man in charge explained a little bit about the Buddhist religion for tourists, and then ended his talk by telling them he had something to say to them that they would never forget—and I have never forgotten it. It was a proverb of the Buddhist religion:

'To every man is given the key to the gates of heaven;
the same key opens the gates of hell.'

What, then, is the value of the key to heaven? It is true that if we lack clear instructions that determine which is the gate to heaven and which the gate to hell, the key may be a dangerous object to use.

Atom bomb mushroom over Hiroshima

Hiroshima after the bomb   The Gembakou observatory

(In seconds more than 200,000 dead men, women, and children, victims of Hiroshima and Nagasaki atom bombs)

But it obviously has value. How can we enter heaven without it? The instructions, also, would be of no value without the key. So it is evident that, in spite of the fact that science could produce enormous horror in the world, it is of value because it can produce something.

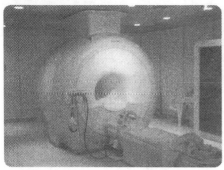 

MRI   Hubble space telescope

Another value of science is the fun called intellectual enjoyment which some people get from reading and learning and thinking about it, and which others get from working in it. This is a very real and important point and one which is not considered enough by those who tell us it is our social responsibility to reflect on the impact of science on society.

Is this mere personal enjoyment of value to society as a whole? No! But it is also a responsibility to consider the value of society itself. Is it, in the last analysis, to arrange things so that people can enjoy things? If so, the enjoyment of science is as important as anything else.

While a student at the Aspropyrgos Academy, I (at left) and my classmate Kostas Stasis in a lecture on humankind's first space satellite (1957).

But I would like not to underestimate the value of the worldview which is the result of scientific effort. We have been led to imagine all sorts of things infinitely more marvelous than the imaginings of poets and dreamers of the past. It shows that the imagination of nature is far, far greater than the imagination of man. For instance, how much more remarkable it is for us to be stuck half of us upside down by a mysterious attraction, to a spinning ball that has been swinging in space for billions of years, than to be carried on the back of an elephant supported on a tortoise swimming in a bottomless sea?

The mysterious attraction

I have thought about these things so many times alone that I hope you will excuse me if I remind you of some thoughts that I am sure you have all had—or this type of thought—which no one could ever have had in the past, because people then didn't have the information we have about the world today.

For instance, I stand at the seashore, alone, and start to think.

There are the rushing waves
mountains of molecules,
each stupidly minding its own business . . .
trillions apart . . .
yet forming white surf in unison.

Ages on ages . . .
before any eyes could see . . .
year after year . . .
thunderously pounding the shore as now.
For whom, for what? . . .
on a dead planet,
with no life to entertain.

Never at rest . . .
tortured by energy . . .
wasted prodigiously by the sun . . .
poured into space.
A mite makes the sea roar.

Deep in the sea,
all molecules repeat
the patterns of one another
till complex new ones are formed.
They make others like themselves . . .
and a new dance starts.

Growing in size and complexity . . .
living things,
masses of atoms,
DNA, protein . . .

dancing a pattern ever more intricate.
Out of the cradle
onto the dry land . . .
here it is standing . . .
atoms with consciousness . . .
matter with curiosity.

Stands at the sea . . .
wonders at wondering . . . I . . .
a universe of atoms . . .
an atom in the universe.

The same thrill, the same awe and mystery, come again and again when we look at any problem deeply enough. With more knowledge comes deeper, more wonderful mystery, luring one on to penetrate deeper still. Never concerned that the answer may prove disappointing, but with pleasure and confidence we turn over each new stone to find unimagined strangeness leading on to more wonderful questions and mysteries—certainly a grand adventure!

It is true that few unscientific people have this particular type of religious experience. Our poets do not write about it; our artists do not try to portray this remarkable thing. I don't know why. Is nobody inspired by our present picture of the universe? The value of science remains unsung by singers, so you are reduced to hearing—not a song or a poem, but an evening lecture about it.

This is not yet a scientific age.

Perhaps one of the reasons is that you have to know how to read the music. For instance, the scientific article says, perhaps, something like this: 'The radioactive phosphorus content of the cerebrum of the rat decreases to one-half in a period of two weeks.' Now, what does that mean?

It means that phosphorus that is in the brain of a rat (and also in mine, and yours) is not the same phosphorus as it was two weeks ago, but that all of the atoms that are in the brain are being replaced, and the ones that were there before have gone away.

So what is this mind, what are these atoms with consciousness? Last week's potatoes! That is what now can remember what was going on in my mind a year ago—a mind which has long ago been replaced.

This is what it means when one discovers how long it takes for the atoms of the brain to be replaced by other atoms, to note that the thing which I call my individuality is only a pattern or dance. The atoms come into my brain, dance a dance, then go out; always new atoms but always doing the same dance, remembering what the dance was yesterday.

When we read about this in the newspaper, it says, 'The scientist says that this discovery may have importance in the cure of cancer.' The paper is only interested in the use of the idea, not the idea itself. Hardly anyone can understand the importance of the idea, it is so remarkable. Except that, possibly, some children catch on. And when a child catches on to an idea like that, we have a scientist. These ideas do filter down (in spite of all the conversation about TV replacing thinking), and lots of kids get the spirit—and when they have the spirit you have a scientist. It's too late for them to get the spirit when they are in our universities, so we must attempt to explain these ideas to children.

Introducing science to children at young age

I would now like to turn to a third value that science has. It is a little more indirect, but not much. The scientist has a lot of experience with ignorance and doubt and uncertainty, and this experience is of very great importance, I think. When a scientist doesn't know the answer to a problem, he is ignorant. When he has a hunch as to what the result is, he is uncertain. And when he is pretty darn sure of what the result is going to be, he is in some doubt. We have found it of paramount importance that in order to progress we must recognize the ignorance and leave room for doubt. Scientific knowledge is a body of statements of varying degrees of certainty—some most unsure, some nearly sure, none *absolutely* certain.

Now, we scientists are used to this, and we take it for granted that it is perfectly consistent to be unsure that it is possible to live and *not* know. But I don't know whether everyone realizes that this is true. Our freedom to doubt was born of a struggle against authority in the early days of science. It was a very deep and strong struggle. Permit us to question—to doubt, that's all—not to be sure. And I think it is important that we do not forget the importance of this struggle and thus perhaps lose what we have gained. Here lies a responsibility to society.

The murder of Hypatia by a mob of Christian fanatics. (Ironically, Bishop Cyril, who instigated the murder, was canonized as saint).

We are all sad when we think of the wondrous potentialities human beings seem to have, as contrasted with their small accomplishments. Again and again people have thought that we could do much better. They of the past saw in the nightmare of their times a dream for the future. We, of their future, see that their dreams, in certain ways surpassed, have in many ways remained dreams. The hopes for the future today are, in good share, those of yesterday.

Once some thought that the possibilities people had were not developed because most of these people were ignorant. With education universal, could all men be Voltaires?

The philosopher Voltaire

Bad can be taught at least as efficiently as good.

Education is a strong force, but for either good or evil.

Communications between nations must promote understanding: So went another dream. But the machines of communication can be channeled or choked. What is communicated can be truth or lie. Communication is a strong force also, but for either good or bad.

The applied scientists should free men of material problems at least. Medicine controls diseases. And the record here seems all to the good. Yet there are men patiently working to create great plagues and poisons. They are to be used in warfare tomorrow.

Atom bomb   Chemical bomb

Nearly everybody dislikes war. Our dream today is peace. In peace, man can develop best the enormous possibilities he seems to have. But maybe future men will find that peace, too, can be good and bad. Perhaps peaceful men will drink out of boredom. Then perhaps drink will become the great problem which seems to keep man from getting all he thinks he should out of his abilities.

Clearly, peace is a great force, as is sobriety, as are material power, communication, education, honesty, and the ideals of many dreamers.

We have more of these forces to control than did the ancients. And maybe we are doing a little better than most of them could do. But what we ought to be able to do seems gigantic compared with our confused accomplishments.

Why is this? Why can't we conquer ourselves?

Because we find that even great forces and abilities do not seem to carry with them clear instructions on how to use them. As an example, the great accumulation of understanding as to how the physical world behaves only convinces one that this behavior seems to have a kind of meaninglessness. The sciences do not directly teach good or bad.

Through all ages men have tried to fathom the meaning of life. They have realized that if some direction or meaning could be given to our actions, great human forces would be unleashed. So, very many answers must have been given to the question of the meaning of it all. But they have been of all different sorts, and the proponents of one answer have looked with horror at the actions of the believers of another. Horror, because from a disagreeing point of view all the great potentialities of the race are being channeled into a false and confining blind alley. In fact, it is from the history of the enormous monstrosities created by false belief that philosophers have realized the apparently infinite and wondrous capacities of human beings.

The Thirty Years' War

St. Bartholomew's Day Massacre
(More than an estimated 100,000 victims in all France)

The dream is to find the open channel.

What, then, is the meaning of it all? What can we say to dispel the mystery of experience?

If we take everything into account, not only what the ancients knew, but all of what we know today that they didn't know, then I think that we must frankly admit that we do not know.

But in admitting this, we have probably found the open channel.

This is not a new idea; this is the idea of the age of reason. This is the philosophy that guided the men who made the democracy that we live under.

The Constitution of the United States

The idea that no one really knew how to run a government led to the idea that we should arrange a system by which new ideas could be developed, tried out, tossed out, more new ideas brought in; a trial and error system. This method was a result of the fact that science was already showing itself to be a successful venture at the end of the 18th century. Even then it was clear to socially minded people that the openness of the possibilities was an opportunity, and that doubt and discussion were essential to progress into the unknown. If we want to solve a problem that we have never solved before, we must leave the door to the unknown ajar.

We are at the very beginning of time for the human race. It is not unreasonable that we grapple with problems. There are tens of thousands of years in the future. Our responsibility is to do what we can, learn what we can, improve the solutions and pass them on. It is our responsibility to leave the men of the future a free hand. In the impetuous youth of humanity, we can make grave errors that can stunt our growth for a long time. This we will do if we say we have the answers now, so young and ignorant; if we suppress all discussion, all criticism, saying, 'This is it, boys, man is saved!' and thus doom man for a long time to the chains of authority, confined to the limits of our present imagination.

It has been done so many times before.

Socrates taking the hemlock

Galileo's trial

Giordano Bruno

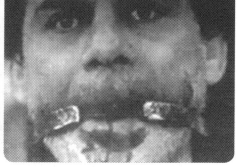

Depiction of Bruno with gag on the stake

It is our responsibility as scientists, knowing the great progress and great value of a satisfactory philosophy of ignorance, the great progress that is the fruit of freedom of thought, to proclaim the value of this freedom, to teach how doubt is not to be feared but welcomed and discussed, and to demand this freedom as our duty to all coming generations.

As a child and teenager, I experienced two insane wars. The first was World War II, which lasted from 1939 until 1945, and a Greek Civil War that lasted from 1945 to 1959.

I witnessed the war atrocities such as public executions, the burning of houses as reprisals, and other insanities of humankind. Later on, when I studied history, science, and philosophy, I became an ardent antiwar proponent. I admired Mahatma Gandhi, who liberated India from the British rule through nonviolence and the philosopher Bernard Russell, Albert Einstein, and others who championed the antiwar movement and especially the nonproliferation of nuclear weapons.

When in 2003 the moron president of the United States George W. Bush was ready to declare war against Iraq, students from the University of Miami (the Greens) invited me to speak at one of their antiwar rallies. I accepted the invitation and gave them an antiwar speech

At a rally against the Iraq war

Greetings

First, I would like to congratulate the Greens for being part of the worldwide movement against the insanity of war.

Wars have been the scourge of humankind since the dawn of history, but nothing is more obscene today than war with modern conventional weapons, not to mention nuclear, chemical or bacteriological means of destruction.

Mark Twain, the great American thinker, stated (and I quote):

> *Man is the only animal that deals in the atrocity of atrocities, war. He is the only one that gathers his brethren about him and goes forth in cold blood and calm pulse to exterminate his kind. He is the only animal that for sordid wages will march out . . . and help to slaughter strangers of his own species who have done him no harm and with whom he has no quarrel . . . . And in the intervals between campaigns he washes the blood off his hands and works for 'the universal brotherhood of man'—with his mouth.*

Shall we ever learn from the horrible business of war?

Now the war drums are again reverberating from Washington and, as often is the case, religion, and nationalism are used to fuel the flames. War is a business in which men and now women are sent to die so that others might be rich or richer.

George W. Bush and his warmongers are telling us that we are in a state of war with terrorism, and with this pretext our civil rights have been eroded. Now he wants us to go to war with Iraq in defiance of the United Nation's Security Council.

George W. Bush, although he sent Colin Power to the United Nations, repeatedly stated that with or without the consent of the United Nation's Security Council, we will attack Iraq to topple Saddam Hussein's government or, as he stated, to bring a regime change. This statement by itself is a violation of international law. It is the same as if an individual petitioned the courts to restrain a neighbor whom he fears, and the courts refuse to grant him the request, he then proceeds by disregarding the court and taking the law in his hand by shooting his perceived enemy to death.

Naturally, he will be found guilty of murder, as our country will be condemned by the international community if George W. Bush would be allowed to proceed with his war plans.

George W. Bush and his warmonger secretary of defense Rumsfeld, the same person who offered Saddam Hussein a pair of silver spurs when he was our friend and ally, are telling us that war with sophisticated smart weapons will have limited civilian casualties. This is another oxymoron and obscene statement. This statement with George W. Bush and Rumsfeld's illogic, is telling us that it is permissible to kill thousands of people as long as they are in uniform. We buried alive thousands of Iraqis during the Gulf war with 'sophisticated' bombs which sucked the air or oxygen causing their asphyxiation without having a chance of fighting back. Now, the warmongers are telling us, the new weapons are one hundred percent more effective.

My question to those warmongers is: don't members of the military have families; don't they have mothers, fathers, brothers, and sisters, lovers, or children of their own? The answer of course is yes. Simply, soldiers on both sides of wars are pawns in the hands of the war maniacs who profit from their death.

George W. Bush brands other nations as terrorist nations or the 'axis of evil.' Is it not true that our country has the largest stockpile of nuclear, chemical, and bacteriological weapons of mass destruction? Are we not the number one exporters of killing machines who supplied them to all the brutal dictators, including Saddam Hussein and even bin Laden himself?

Was it not the CIA under the Reagan administration who provided instruction books on how to assassinate foreign leaders, blow up bridges, and bring havoc to other countries because we don't like their form of government?

Didn't our greedy capitalists replace the pre-World War II colonial powers and subject most of the third world poor nations to modern day slavery?

Yes, perhaps Iraq and many other countries need regime changes, but that is not our problem. It is the decision and responsibility of their citizens.

Do we need a regime change as well? The answer is again yes, but this change should come not with weapons and killing but with the power of our vote. This is the only way to bring change and enlightenment to our country to regain the respect of the world community of nations.

Closing, I would like to bring your attention to the United Nations Declaration of Human Rights. Article I states:

> All human beings are born free and equal in dignity and rights. They are *endowed* with *reason* and *conscience* and should act towards one another in a spirit of brotherhood.

Although I subscribe to the principles of this article, as an atheist I reject the idea that we are endowed by an omnipotent, omniscient creator or god as many are interpreting the above.

It is us, the species *Homo sapiens* and no supernatural powers that set the standards and laws for a peaceful coexistence and justice for all. If the above statement is true, wars, slavery, and segregation would never have taken place. That is why I am urging you, the youth of our nation, to always question authority no matter from where it comes. It is up to you, the new generation to bring the profound lyrics of John Lennon's 'Imagine' to reality. Perhaps now is the time to declare his dream:

> *Nothing to kill or die*
> *for And no religion too . . .*
> *You may say that I'm a*
> *dreamer But I'm not the*
> *only one*

And to you, the Greens, I would like to remind you of an East African proverb:

> *When the elephants fight, it is the grass that suffers.*

Thank you.
Christos Tzanetakos
Founder, Atheists of Florida, Inc.

*   *   *

I was vigilant and ready to take action whenever the government violated the First Amendment of the U.S. Constitution. Alice stood by my side for all of my activities, and she even took part in street protests and marches.

Alice at a peaceful protest

Alice and I, although both staunch atheists, are against proselytizing for atheism. We perceive all believers of any faith victims of their dogmas. Nevertheless, we are adherent to Emile Zola's statement:

> *Civilization will thrive when the last stone From the last church falls on the last priest.*

Epilogue

Today, "the year of our Lord and savior" 2010, wars are raging and genocides, hunger, and the deterioration of the planet are rampant.

In spite of this, religious leaders from all faiths and denominations are still holding their holy books, written thousands of years ago by ignorant shamans, proclaiming:

My friends, here are all the answers you have to know!

"Praise the omnipotent, omniscient Lord"

Iraq War   War in Afghanistan

Khmer Rouge genocide   Rwanda genocide

When will we ever learn?

We are indeed very far from a true scientific era.

Christos Tzanetakos

Appendix

On August 25, 1992, John B. Massen, who had formed the San Francisco Atheists Region, incorporated in California a new organization called Atheists Alliance, Inc.

The scope of the new organization was to bring all democratically organized atheists under one umbrella. He invited Atheists of Florida, Minnesota Atheists, Atheists Coalition of San Diego, Atheists United of Los Angeles, and Atheists and Agnostics of Wisconsin to join the Alliance.

I flew to Los Angeles and was elected co-president of the new organization. I served as president for two consecutive terms and at the end of my second year, we had acquired five more member organizations under the umbrella of Atheists Alliance.

Today, in 2011, the organization became international with members from all around the world. I, along with the founders of the original member organizations, am a pioneer of modern atheism.

Atheist Alliance Member Organizations

ARGENTINA
Association Civil De Ateos (Buenos Aires)

AUSTRALIA
Atheist Foundation of Australia

AUSTRIA
Allianz Fuer Humanismus und Atheismus (Linz)

CANADA
Humanist Association of Canada (Ontario/Manitoba/Saskatchewan/Alberta/British Columbia)
Kamloops Center for Rational Thought (British Columbia)
Niagara Secular Humanists (Ontario)

DENMARK
Dansk Ateistisk Selskab (Danish Atheist Society) (Kovenhavn)

FINLAND
Atheist Association of Finland (Helsinki)

GERMANY
International League of Non-Religious and Atheists (IBKA) (Hagen)

ICELAND
SAMT-Samfelag Trulausra-The Atheist Society (Reykjavik)

IRELAND
Atheist Ireland (Dublin)

INDIA
Atheist Center (Vijayawada)
Traksheel (Rationalist) Society/Punjap) (Reqd) (Punjab)

MALAWI
Association of Secular Humanists (Longwe)

NIGERIA
Nigerian Humanists Movement (Lagos)

PORTUGUAL
Portal Ateu—Movimento Ateista Portugues (Lisbon)

UGANDA
Atheist Association of Uganda (Kampala)

Within the United States

CALIFORNIA
Atheists and Other Freethinkers (Sacramento)
Atheists United (Los Angeles)
Central Valley Alliance of Atheists & Skeptics (Fresno)
Humanist Society of Santa Barbara (Santa Barbara)

COLORADO
Boulder Atheists (Boulder)
Boulder Heretics (Boulder)
Freethinkers of Colorado Springs (Colorado Springs)
Humanists of Colorado (Denver)

DISTRICT OF COLUMBIA
Washington Area Secular Humanists (Washington, DC)

FLORIDA
Atheists of Florida (Tampa)

GEORGIA
Atlanta Freethought Society (Atlanta)

IOWA
Iowa Atheists & Freethinkers (Iowa City)

KANSAS
Atheist Community of Topeka (Topeka)

LOUISIANA
New Orleans Secular Humanists Association (New Orleans)

MINNESOTA
Atheists for Human Rights (Minneapolis)
Campus Atheists and Secular Humanists (Minneapolis)
University of Minnesota (Minneapolis)
Central Minnesota Friends Free of Theism (St. Cloud)
Minnesota Atheists (Minneapolis)

MISSOURI
Rationalist Society of St. Louis (St. Louis)

NEW MEXICO
Atheists and Freethinkers of New Mexico (Albuquerque)

NORTH CAROLINA
Charlotte Atheists & Agnostics (Charlotte)

OKLAHOMA
Oklahoma Atheists (Oklahoma City)

PENNSYLVANIA
Freethought Society (Philadelphia)
Pennsylvania Nonbelievers (York/Lancaster/Harrisburg)

SOUTH CAROLINA
The Secular Humanists of the Low Country (Charleston)

TENNESSEE
Rationalists of East Tennessee (Knoxville)

TEXAS
Atheist Community of Austin (Austin)
Freethinkers Association of Central Texas (San Antonio)
Metroplex Atheists (Ft. Worth/Dallas)

WISCONSIN
Atheists and Agnostics of Wisconsin (Madison)
Southeast Wisconsin Freethinkers (Milwaukee)

Acknowledgments

Thanks to my friend Joseph Goldman for his many hours spent proofreading, correcting my grammar, and checking the book for formatting and consistency.

Finally, my thanks go to my parents, teachers, professors, and all the giants of human thought whose works and ideas have shaped and guided my life.

Christos Tzanetakos